Praise for *The Resilience Plan*

"*The Resilience Plan* is highly valuable for a pair of reasons. First, it convincingly identifies resilience as a necessary trait for surviving and thriving in today's frenetic world. Second, it not only shows the importance of having a strategic resilience plan, but also details the specific form the plan should take. It's not to be missed."

ROBERT CIALDINI, *New York Times*–bestselling author of *Influence* and *Pre-Suasion*

"This gem of a book draws on best practices from both psychology and business. *The Resilience Plan* guides busy professionals and leaders step-by-step in the creation of a personal plan to reduce burnout and boost resilience. Unlike some books, it takes into account actual work-life demands and resources. Marie-Hélène Pelletier delivers on her promise to show you how to boost your resilience and mental health in just a few minutes a day. Use this book to enjoy a better year ahead!"

CHRISTINE A. PADESKY, coauthor *of Mind Over Mood*

"In today's competitive marketplace, it's not enough for leaders to simply do their job well. In *The Resilience Plan*, Marie-Hélène Pelletier expertly weaves science and story to help leaders build a custom resilience plan based on individual priorities and the context they live and work in."

DORIE CLARK, *Wall Street Journal*–bestselling author of *The Long Game* and executive education faculty at Columbia Business School

"Marie-Hélène Pelletier provides a practical, inspiring, and engaging reflection on resilience. Pelletier anchors her perspectives in a deep understanding of psychological theory and research, and weaves engaging anecdotes from her personal and professional life that animate the core ideas. *The Resilience Plan* is a delight to read, a source of insight, and a valuable resource for addressing the challenges of work-life in the twenty-first century."

MICHAEL LEITER, coauthor of *The Burnout Challenge*

"An inspiring and practical book that can aid leaders, managers, and participants in any organization and help them navigate and cope with their ever-changing work environment. Having spent many years focused on management education and research, particularly at UBC and INSEAD, I have witnessed first-hand the personal challenges managers and professionals face in a complex world that demands peak performance. The need for individuals to proactively address their own resilience and contribute to the resilience of others has never been more pronounced. *The Resilience Plan* provides a comprehensive framework for building individual and organizational resilience and should be at the top of your reading list."

DANIEL MUZYKA, Dean and Professor Emeritus at UBC Sauder School of Business

"Marie-Hélène Pelletier has written a transfixing playbook on how to truly optimize your work and health. Combined with real-life experiences, each page is packed with practical yet empowering strategies to help build your plan for resilience. From rethinking your supply and demands to how to lead with priority values, Pelletier gets you crafting a balanced path to success. A must-read for any leader!"

SARIKA GUNDU, MSC, Director of Canadian Health and Welfare Benefits at BMO Financial Group

"Through storytelling and practical wisdom, Marie-Hélène Pelletier helps us see past the stories we tell ourselves about our own resilience. Whether you're a leader or someone others rely on, do us all a favor and read this before you burn out."

MARY ANN BAYNTON, author of *Mindful Manager* and *Keeping Well at Work*

"*The Resilience Plan* is a must-read for both new and existing leaders. Marie-Hélène Pelletier's easy-to-read book seamlessly integrates psychology and business to provide leaders with invaluable insights and strategies for instilling optimism, a can-do mindset, and the ability to differentiate with even more resilience."

GARY LATHAM, Professor of Organizational Behavior at the Rotman School of Management, University of Toronto

"As someone who has written about the importance of adapting and bouncing back from adversity in my own book, *Driven to Succeed: From Poverty to Podium*, I highly recommend Marie-Hélène Pelletier's *The Resilience Plan*. She convincingly argues that resilience is not a given; it's a skill that can be developed and strengthened with practice. Pelletier shows you the way."

KENDAL NETMAKER, entrepreneur and international keynote speaker

"A must-read! *The Resilience Plan* is an indispensable guide for those navigating high-demand workplaces, effectively dispelling misconceptions about burnout and resilience. Personal and practical, the book provides insightful advice on building resilience plans, fortified with compelling data, case studies, and anecdotes. Whether you're teetering on the brink of burnout or seeking to reinforce your resilience, *The Resilience Plan* is a game-changing resource in the realm of mental health and work performance management."

DR. STEFANIE ROBEL, Associate Professor of Neuroscience at the University of Alabama at Birmingham

"We all need resilience now in this world of constant and disruptive change. *The Resilience Plan* shows us how to build resilience by providing inspiration, frameworks, and practical steps. Through a mix of psychology, strategic savvy, and illuminating personal experiences, Marie-Hélène Pelletier helps us work through adversity and find the way to growth."

GENA COX, PhD, author of *Leading Inclusion*

"Marie-Hélène Pelletier has crafted an excellent guidebook on building and nurturing resilience. She weaves personal, anecdotal experiences with the latest research on creating a repertoire of resilience skills, including easy-to-follow, practical exercises. This is a very readable book."

ROBERT WILSON, PhD, former CEO of Wilson Banwell Human Solutions

"A must-read book for all professionals and leaders interested in learning how to align work performance with psychological health and well-being. Marie-Hélène Pelletier clearly has a deep and broad understanding of her subject matter and an uncanny ability to inspire professionals and leaders to take action and get results."

DR. JANEL GAUTHIER, Professor Emeritus of Psychology at Laval University

"Every CEO and leader knows that mental health is a growing challenge—and an opportunity—but how does one build resilience? In this regard, Marie-Hélène Pelletier's *The Resilience Plan* couldn't be more timely. She offers us a very human, empathetic, and pragmatic approach to resilience, one grounded in psychology and refined through her extensive real-world work experience. We can all see ourselves in this book, and that's a good thing."

DEAN CONNOR, Corporate Director; retired President and CEO of Sun Life Financial

THE
RESILIENCE
PLAN

THE
RESILIENCE
PLAN

A Strategic Approach to Optimizing Your
Work Performance and Mental Health

MARIE-HÉLÈNE PELLETIER, PhD, MBA

PAGE TWO

Cataloguing in publication information is available from Library and Archives Canada.
ISBN 978-1-77458-366-1 (paperback)
ISBN 978-1-77458-367-8 (ebook)

Page Two
pagetwo.com

Edited by Emily Schultz
Copyedited by Jenny Govier
Proofread by Alison Strobel
Cover design by Peter Cocking and Taysia Louie
Interior design by Peter Cocking and Setareh Ashrafologhalai
Printed and bound in Canada by Friesens
Distributed in Canada by Raincoast Books
Distributed in the US and internationally by Macmillan

24 25 26 27 28   5 4 3 2 1

drmarie-helene.com

To all leaders and professionals, current and future. May this book save you time and keep you fabulous—so you can enjoy even more of your professional and personal lives. And may your edge get even sharper as you become strategic about your resilience.

Contents

—[1]—
You're Fabulous and At Risk

As soon as I step into the river, the current grabs my legs and pulls me off my feet. The force is so strong, I have no control. The river roars and rushes around me.

I can't beat it. I am at the river's mercy.

My husband, Nic, and I love mountaineering, and we had embarked on an eight-day traverse in the Canadian Rockies. Seven days earlier, at the end of day one, we had come upon this same river. It rushed down from the mountain and was just wide enough that we would have to take about a dozen steps in it. We came up with a plan to get across based on our strengths. Nic went first, then me. It was difficult, but we made it.

Now, as the river decides my fate, everything slips into slow motion. I see myself standing on the other side of the riverbank, feeling victorious. Depleted after days on the trail, that memory seems years behind me.

We had started out on snow-packed trails. The farther up, the less snow we ran into, until eventually there was no snow and no river, which meant soon we would be out of water. I began to get dizzy from dehydration. Nic and I did everything we could to help me keep going, but by day four, we had no choice but to turn back. I couldn't will myself to keep going, and I hated it. It was almost worse than the dehydration.

At day eight, we were exhausted and barely speaking because we were in self-preservation mode. We arrived back at the river again, and it was higher from melting snow, and more tumultuous. Not being able to hear each other over the sound of the rushing water, we could only wave and sign at each other. Nic went first again and gestured that he would come back for me.

"No!" I shouted fruitlessly and pointed. "Stay there. I'll come to you."

That was the last thing I said before the river pulled me in.

Where I was once confident and strong, now I was paralyzed with fear.

Will the rushing currents knock me against the rocks?
Does Nic see me? What if he can't get to me?
I might drown.

Suddenly, a force grabbed me by my backpack and threw me out of the water on the other side of the river. It was Nic, of course. We sat on the ground catching our breath and staring at each other. We knew what could have happened—that could have been my last day.

I learned an important lesson at the river that day. The biggest difference between day one and day eight was not the river—it was us. By day eight, we had abandoned the strategies that had kept us safe. We had divided. We had tried to do it on our own. We—I—just assumed that we would be able to face whatever happened.

It works the same way in our work life. Most of us have an eye on our resilience when things are mostly fine, like on day one; we can be very good. Where we get caught is on day eight—when more things are going on, and we have more, unexpected, and larger demands, and we are not as attentive to what we need to do to stay resilient.

You're Already There

You're already at day eight. You are at risk of burnout, exhaustion, or being swept away by the forceful currents of your personal and work life. I know this because, as a doctoral-level registered psychologist with an MBA who has focused on workplace mental health for my entire career, I have mostly found myself working with professionals and leaders. I have seen the impact of ever-increasing demands in the absence of deliberate attention to resilience. Initially, alertness, ability to make decisions, and concentration appear to be exactly the same—or even better. Yet, all these are getting taxed. You just don't see it yet. If the demands continue, then you may see the impact. For example, some things fall through the cracks, you make a sub-optimal judgment call (which you typically don't do), or you need to re-read a document because your mind can't stay focused. These are early signs to pay attention to, but you ignore them because you have no time.

As accomplished high achievers, we tell ourselves we can handle it, and we keep telling ourselves this even when the demands on us change. The reality is that you are likely already affected by all the demands you face, whether it is marginally, moderately, or significantly. You're already there. It's not your fault, and it is understandable.

You also may not put much stock in your own wellness. Sacrifices must be made, after all. You know that you should eat healthier, get more sleep, exercise, and see friends. First, you don't have time. Second, and most importantly, whenever you've done these things, nothing changed. And you've tried looking at the situation from various perspectives. You are resourceful and solution oriented. Still, nothing changes.

Here are some comments I've heard in my individual coaching sessions, team coaching sessions, and events where I've presented:

I always tell myself I can push through.

I'll do self-care when I have time.

I can't have anxiety or stress, so I just ignore it.

I don't need to focus on my needs because I am strong.

The work culture is the problem.

These comments are not just coming from my clients. I have also fully believed each of these before. Particularly being a psychologist, I have, for example, in the past assumed more internal power to change things than what was realistic in certain contexts, and I have been burned.

Most professionals and leaders assume they are resilient and don't need to do anything about it. And yet, the river rises. What you can handle one day may become impossible down the road. The truth is, you can't wing self-care or will yourself to be resilient. You need a custom mental health strategy around your personal life and work life.

Resilience Is Not a Given

Matt works in a senior role in finance. Without realizing it fully, he had come to believe that resilience is who he is, that it is part of his personality. Therefore, he did not think he needed to do anything to improve it. In fact, he shared with me that doing anything about it would probably be a waste of time.

To Matt, addressing his mental health seemed like a version of the law of diminishing returns, a theory in economics that predicts that after some optimal level of capacity is reached, adding an additional factor of production will result in smaller increases in output. Yet, he had been feeling anxious for the past six months—not just the usual stress that comes and goes, but a more intense anxiety. What is key here is that, given the continuous stream of demands that were coming his way, it was more probable than not that he had tipped over to the other side of "optimal level of capacity"—and he had been ignoring it. His optimistically biased belief got in the way, and in fact put him and many others at risk. These risks may include a lower quality of work, professional errors, and inadequate understanding and support of others. Yet, some of these demands can be predicted and even managed, at times proactively. I helped Matt see that resilience and mental health can often be nurtured and improved.

Resilience is not a personality trait. We are not born or made resilient due to circumstances, although circumstances can influence it. A most commonly accepted definition of resilience is our ability to go through adversity and come out even stronger. While resilience has been associated with certain personality traits like optimism, for example, it varies within one person across time and situations. This means we can affect it, and in fact we should invest in it, nourish it.

Given enough demands, anyone can burn out. This makes sense, yet you likely still think it could never be you. What is missed by most professionals and leaders is a realistic understanding of the demands they face and attention to what's coming. You've been valued, praised, recognized for your ability to take things on, and to some degree, you have identified with this role. The reality is that demands become larger, more complex, and unexpected. They cannot be met by putting your head down and working smarter. They cannot be met by maintaining a "yes" approach that you believe is selective but is not. These and most of what you've tried so far put you at risk of imbalance. Given the same amount of supply, additional demands eventually won't work.

Resilience is not a given. You need a strategy.

A Strategic Resilience Plan Is Good Business

NAV CANADA's largest segment of employees is air traffic services personnel, including air traffic controllers and flight service specialists who work at over a hundred staffed sites across the country. These include air traffic control towers, area control centers, flight service stations, and flight information centers. This unique group of professionals who keep

Canada's skies safe are hard to find and hard to replace, and they play a critical role in a high-stakes environment.

Lyne Wilson is responsible for human resources activities within the organization from both an operational and a strategic perspective. She championed mental health in the workplace by developing a mental health strategy in 2009 and implementing a peer support program, Light the Way, in October 2012, and I have had the chance to know and work with Lyne since then. In speaking with her recently, she stressed, "A mental health strategy can't just be an HR program or an HR strategy. It has to be part of the business strategy."

This also applies to individuals and their need to have their own mental health strategy. Professionals and leaders can't just think of it as a part of their personal life. It has to be part of their overall life.

Doris Hawaleshka, an HR executive who has worked with various organizations across several industries, wishes that professionals and leaders would begin putting their hands up sooner when they are not in a good place. She finds that many resist getting help and assume invincibility.

I have seen this in my work. Our own mental health can easily remain off our radar, a blind spot. One of the reasons businesses benefit from having a strategic plan for their business goals is that it forces them to look at their idea from various angles so they don't miss blind spots, ensuring that perspectives and forces influencing the context are considered and accounted for. For example, an entrepreneur may have the goal of starting a professional services business. Building a strategic plan would force them to clarify their offering, analyze what similar offerings are already in the market, and establish what their new venture's values are and what its strengths, weaknesses, opportunities, and threats may be. This produces strategic pillars and actions and a map that guides where actions will be focused and where they won't, given a specific goal and limited resources. It customizes their approach. A strategic plan focused on our resilience can do the same for us individually.

The Common Approach May Not Be Your Best Approach

Your current approach to your own resilience is probably not a plan and is unlikely customized. Given the many demands you face, and in the absence of a professional by your side helping plan, monitor, and optimize your resilience (the way you may have a hairstylist, a dentist, and a physician or nurse practitioner), you don't have much time and you don't have someone on your team whose role it is to manage your resilience plan. You don't necessarily need the regular check-in with a registered psychologist, but in the absence of a plan, the chances of you optimizing your situation are left in the open and can become a liability.

Likewise, you can't just adopt someone else's plan or follow guidance you hear from a friend or in the media. For example, if you hear, "You should exercise more," that may be true, but it's too generic. What's best for you and your needs?

You may assume you are resilient and don't need to do anything about it.

When I asked my client Beth how confident she was about her strategic resilience plan, she said, "I'm a 5 out of 10."

"What do you do to protect and build your resilience?" I asked.

"I exercise a few times a week, when I can."

"So, in the past week, how many times?"

"The past few months have been exceptionally busy, so not much," Beth explained. "But in general, probably two to three times per week. And I went for a massage last month."

I have heard versions of this response many times, including from myself. The top traps professionals and leaders fall into are not having clarity on which actions are key and not maintaining them in times of high demand.

Beth knows exercise is good for her and tries to walk about three days per week. Except she doesn't walk when it's raining, or if she needs to work extra, or if a call keeps her at her desk a bit longer. She's fairly confident in her work but worries about her ability to maintain the quality of her reports until retirement, given the increasingly complex and demanding nature of the mandates she is given.

What Beth has is one action—one action, not a plan. It's actually a good place to start. Starting with one action often leads to some momentum that then can be useful to eventually design a plan. But ultimately, she needs a custom plan. If not, she runs the risk of just implementing this one action that is not necessarily optimized to produce the desired outcome. Her plan will start with her goal and will ensure that specific and customized directions and actions (strategies and actions) are identified, to then be implemented.

You need a plan, and you need it to be personal to you. The generic idea, "To be resilient, we should all be physically active, so that's my plan," does not cut it. Ideally, your plan will include three to five pillars that will help you improve resilience. Beth's strategic resilience plan now includes one of three key pillars focused on self-care. Within this pillar, one of her actions is a fifteen-minute walk three times a week. So she went from the generic, "I should exercise," to the following: "Given my goal of increasing resilience and my context in which I currently lack self-care, one of my pillars is now 'self-care,' within which I have the action of going for a fifteen-minute walk three days per week between five and six p.m." You need a plan that is personal to you in your current context: a strategic plan. This is something I learned first-hand during my training.

Context Is Everything

During the very first week of my MBA program at the University of British Columbia, I had a feeling I didn't belong there. It was a rigorous, top-notch program in which I was one of the very few women, the only student who was a speaker of French as first language, and the only psychologist.

Jammed into an amphitheater, the other three hundred students looked as though they dealt with spreadsheets and money all day. Some wore ties. I had completed advanced graduate-level statistics in my training, but financial statements and accounting could not be further from anything I had spent my life training for.

We were divided into teams of four and given the weekend to do all the financial analysis of a hypothetical organization and then make a recommendation to the organization on whether to proceed with a costly new product. We could do all the analysis we wanted as a team, but we then had to write a report with our recommendations individually.

Our team worked all weekend, all day, and all night, taking shifts on accounting and Excel spreadsheets and analysis. The assignment initially looked easy enough. Then, as we progressed, things became uncertain. The more we made clever models, the more we saw it: If the organization proceeded with what they were planning to do, they would make a massive profit. We were solid, golden. We had the information we needed, we had broadened our analyses, and we knew what to do. My group members excitedly buzzed about recommending "a go" for the lucrative proposed venture and raved about profit margins. We'd seen the numbers. It would work.

We each went our own way to write our report. I headed back to my apartment, still a bit dizzy from all the analyses. I sat down, pulled out my notebooks, and poured a fresh cup of coffee. Maybe this MBA program would be easier than I thought.

As I began to write my report, I ran the numbers again. This time, I considered the fuller context. I started to think the venture would *not* work. This type of product, at this price, in this economic context in this country, considering the core business of the organization, was just not going to fly. A pit of anxiety formed in my stomach. I had a huge decision to make: Go with the flow and my team or strike out on my own and spotlight this whole other part of the picture. The second option required potentially making an unpopular recommendation that would likely not generate an "A" and could cause conflict with my group.

In the amphitheater for the next class, the professors stood at the bottom and faced us. We sat on the edge of our seats as they called on us. Nervous at first, the students became more confident as they recommended proceeding with the venture.

In a tone that seemed to indicate he already knew the answer, one of the professors asked, "Who here recommended a no-go? Who among you concluded that, despite certain data points, when taken in context, this plan may not be the massive financial success it appears to be?"

The air seemed to leave the room. A few rows back I heard some feet shuffling. Three hundred pairs of eyes searched the room. My stomach churned and sweat broke at my hairline. I immediately began to question every decision I had made that had brought me to this point. Who am I to counter these opinions? I am a psychologist, a female ESL psychologist with no accounting depth, in a rigorous MBA program.

I gripped my pencil. As I slowly raised my hand in the packed amphitheater, all eyes turned to me.

"Considering the context, I recommend a no-go. When looking at this company's core business, supply and demand, and the forces impacting the market in this country, I advise not going forward."

"That is the recommended approach," the professor said, smiling.

I lowered my hand as people looked in my direction with whispers and nods of approval. The professor moved on with his lecture, and the students turned to face the blackboard for a lesson on strategy. In that moment, I allowed the realization that would inform my life's work to wash over me: While accounting and financial analyses are critical (and complex), the most effective solutions will also involve looking at the *context* for each company. I had stumbled across strategy as driven by context. This is what made the next steps more likely to succeed.

Language is all about context. It conveys ever-changing cultural subtleties, and it involves timing, relationships, and a confluence of factors that shape the ultimate outcome. I speak English and French; I am often thinking in one and speaking in another. Shifting, slipping, and leaping between linguistic contexts. *Les choses s'entremêlent.* Things are intertwined.

Psychology, too, revels in context. We are trained to consider all elements of the client's context: their environment, socioeconomic factors, culture, and more. We are trained to consider the antecedents. Psychologists are trained to observe, to ask questions and not make assumptions, and to remain open to many possible outcomes. We are trained to understand that things may not be as they appear at first glance, that sometimes there is more to the story that can only be seen when you "zoom out" and take in the larger whole.

The same thing plays out in our lives when it comes to our resilience. We know the numbers, what we should do. This direction is clear: If we exercise five times a week, eat well 80 percent of the time, sleep eight hours, and so on, we will be healthier. "Done," we think. "Just do it." And then we don't. It does not work. Or we actually do all the "things"—we exercise for at least thirty minutes five times a week, we eat well, we see friends and protect our sleep—and that does not work either.

What we need is to consider the reality—the context—of our life in this moment: our values, our sources of energy supply, what demands we have on our energy, and what supports and challenges our efforts to build our resilience. Having the numbers is critical, but it's not enough. We need to take our overall personal context into account. We can't wing it, and it's not a given. We need a strategy.

Your Company's Strategy Is Not Enough

For several reasons, one of which is the human tendency to maintain momentum, most of us will do all we can to avoid having to change anything. Some may tell themselves, "My work is the problem. That is what needs to change, not me." Challenges can come from your work, from you, from the interaction between. Still, regardless of where the cause or causes lie, the person affected is you and the person who will deal with the situation is you. Your plan will need to take your context into account.

Others may tell themselves, "My work strongly supports mental health. I am covered." You may find yourself in the enviable position of working with an employer who is really strong on mental health and offers a variety of wellness programs and resources. And you assume that this covers you enough and you don't need anything else. The resources will be there for you when you need them.

Having access to resources and programs is nice but is not enough. One of the consistent and very hard-to-shift statistics companies notice is the relatively low utilization rate of employee assistance programs (EAPs). Although 30 percent of the working population or more was dealing with some form of mental health challenge prior to the COVID-19 pandemic, we generally observed an average EAP utilization rate of only 8 percent. Part of what explains this is the stigma and self-stigma, a belief that dealing with a mental health challenge labels us negatively (to our employers or peers, but also to ourselves) and that these contexts often involve other variables. The reality is that people still burn out in very strategic and resourced companies, and not everyone burns out in companies that do not offer much support.

If maintaining good mental health were very simple, everyone would have this down pat today. The reality is that we don't. It is not extremely complicated, but work and non-work are systems, with various components and forces affecting each of us uniquely as individuals. We need both the individual and the context in mind, from both psychological and business angles.

The individual is you, with your own values, your personality, your skills, your habits. Your context involves all aspects of your life, work, and non-work, and includes, for example, your relationships, your opportunities for exercise, how much you enjoy your work, and how many leisure activities you have and protect. The psychological angle involves how you think, feel, and react. What I mean by the business angle here is the active and deliberate observation, assessment, and management of the overall context.

Thinking about our workplace mental health in either an individualistic or a systems-only perspective is misleading. Psychology as a field does look at systems at times, but it mostly looks at and works with the depths of the individual. I have not only seen this tendency to focus more on the individualistic perspective first-hand as a psychologist but have also applied this to my own experience and learned that I was wrong. It misses the context. Business does look at the individual, but it mostly looks at the system. This too is important but not sufficient. As an individual looking to lead your own mental health strategically, you need to have an eye on both you as an individual and the context you operate and live in. To succeed at designing, implementing, and reaping the benefits of your strategic resilience plan, you need to incorporate both your individual perspective and the realities of the context you live and work in.

Your Strategic Resilience Plan

You can think about your overall resilience as a ratio of your supply versus your demands. Supply here refers to the ways in which you increase your health and energy. These tend to include healthy lifestyle choices, pleasurable activities, and investing time in what you value. A demand is anything that requires energy from you, whether it is something positive that you have wished for or something negative you would rather not have. Examples of demands include planning a wedding or an international trip, as well as dealing with a workplace conflict or going through a divorce. I refer to this as the "supply-demands ratio." I use "demands" because they are numerous and coming from different sources, and your awareness of all your sources and all the demands within these sources is vital to the success of your strategic resilience plan.

A key to working toward a healthier ratio is having clarity on your overall personal situation. Just telling yourself that you need to meditate (even though you're right; research supports it) isn't sufficient to make it happen. Looking to change and increase every aspect of your self-care is unlikely to be sufficient in a context in which it's not possible to meet your demands. The key is this: *You* are missing from your own plan.

Given that your overall situation involves both you and your context, so in effect multiple variables, having clarity on your situation is necessary for designing your approach. And given that you and your context are complex, your approach likely requires a plan that takes various forces into account. What we need is to bring together elements from psychology and elements from business strategy.

Resilience is not a given. It's a strategy. You need a custom, strategic resilience plan. A plan as unique as your DNA. DNA is a molecule inside your cells that contains the genetic instructions that make you, you. You are likely familiar with the image of the double helix that is DNA.

When I started researching symbols in nature that could help me create a visual model for strategic resilience, I discovered a surprising symmetry with the elements of my framework. Each DNA molecule has two linked strands, like the sides of a ladder. The rungs on that ladder are constructed from four chemical bases. In your strategic resilience plan, you also have two linked strands: your personal life and your professional life. These are the sides of your ladder. And the four bases that form your ladder's rungs are your supply, your demands, your values, and your context.

As you create your strategic resilience plan, you will need to gain insight into those bases:

- Your sources of supply—what gives you energy

- Your sources of demands (positive ones included), both in the present and in the future

- Your values—what is most important to you in life

- Your internal and external contexts and how these influence (both support and challenge) your goal of increased resilience

Strategic resilience double helix.

With all this in mind, you're ready to choose the actions that will make up your strategic resilience plan. If you design your custom workplace mental health plan now, you'll know how to do this forever.

Here's the truly remarkable aspect of the DNA molecule model. As I discovered, the helix is a symbol of resilience. In nature, plants form helixes to get around any impediment to their growth. In other words, they use helixes to thrive despite the challenges of the environment. This is also what your strategic resilience plan will do for you.

Mallory is a very successful professional and leader. She told me that she used to love her work but felt that her calendar had got out of control, and that had been the case for at least six months. She knew what she should do but was not doing it. As she consulted with me and implemented the framework I share in this book, everything changed. To her amazement, creating the plan did not take long, and monthly maintenance takes two minutes. Why does it take just two minutes? Because after her initial reflection, she realized precisely and more realistically where her sources of supply and demands were and the reality of her context, and her values serve as a guide to making choices. She was soon back to her usual energetic self.

"I have clarity," Mallory told me. "I moved from my endless to-do list to a clean '*have*-to-do list' and a '*want*-to-do list,' and I ditched the rest. I implemented my actions, including experimenting with solutions I had dismissed in the past that actually make a material difference, and this is so much better. I wish I had done this six months ago. It's great to have this now moving forward."

By the end of this book, you will have a strategic resilience plan of your own that will give you the edge you need at work and home. With a strategic approach, you can lead your workplace mental health now and into the future, which will have an impact in both your work and personal life. You won't have to will yourself to move forward. You'll be better able to navigate even the most unexpected demands. And you will have more resilience to traverse any terrain, on any day.

Questions for Reflection

- Which idea stayed with you after you finished this chapter?

- What is your goal in reading this book?

Remember

- Being smart, strong, successful, and resourceful is not enough. The immunity you think you have is not real, and the protections you think you have in place are not permanent.

- The solutions you need require a new outlook and approach.

- See your resilience strategically. Designing a custom plan for resiliency will help you in the long run.

- Your plan will consider what brings you energy, your sources of demands, your values, and your context.

- A strategic resilience plan is good business: businesses benefit from having a mental health strategy, and you do too.

- Once you design your strategic resilience plan, you'll know how to do this forever.

—[2]—

Neither Rock nor Wreck

———

You've been told you're the rock. The rock of the family, the rock of the team. You have started to believe it. When you start thinking that you're not doing well, becoming more impatient, concentration going down, no energy, you tell yourself you aren't the rock, you're a wreck. The reality, however, is that you are a human. And as a human, no one is either a rock or a wreck; these are both inanimate things, after all. We're all humans on the continuum of mental health.

The professionals and leaders who have a mental health strategy are typically those who have gone through a burnout in the past or know someone who has. Most people who have not had a burnout don't have a mental health strategy. By putting your head down in the day-to-day, you're at best not learning from past situations and possibly not avoiding future ones. You need to look at the horizon, in both directions.

Your Past Burned-Out Self

I had a finance professional client, I'll call him Jake, who was referred to me by his physician because he was reporting problems with procrastination. As I did my assessment, we both realized that he was showing signs of burnout. His concentration was down, his memory was down, and he was much more impatient than before. He did not have half the energy he used to have and felt disengaged from a role he used to be passionate about, and the amount of "things falling through the cracks" was close to reaching a performance problem.

We looked at the demands Jake faced. There were increases in all his roles: he was involved in full-time work in addition to two committees, had just started volunteer governance work on a board, and also happened to have increased challenges with one of his sons.

Once we talked through all this, we were able to more realistically understand 1) the amount of demands he had in his personal life and in his career, compared to how little supply he had, and 2) the fact that procrastination was not going to be our first focus. Increasing his energy and changing the supply-demands ratio came first. He could then see his situation more clearly and make better decisions.

For some, if nothing changes, things are likely to continue to worsen rather than get better or even stay the same. If you have gone through a burnout in the past few years, ask yourself, "What have I learned from this? What do I know now that would change everything?"

I've heard countless times, from professionals and leaders, "I never thought it would happen to me. It's not me." I often work with senior partners in management consulting firms. They combine the brilliance of their financial acumen with impeccable business and interpersonal skills. Like any of us, given a certain set of circumstances, some find themselves completely burned out. It feels sudden. But it's not. It often also feels scary, and it does not have to.

Here is what I found myself explaining to a management consultant who wondered how on earth they had found themselves completely burned out: Clients often come to them when their organizations are in serious financial trouble. The client is panicked, receiving letters from the bank and facing a sudden financial crisis they did not see coming. However, when the management consultant looks at their financial statements from the past few years, they *do* see the signs—they're all there. And they know how to help.

The day severe anxiety or burnout hits often feels sudden. It's the final straw. Some pain was there prior, but highly capable and resourceful professionals and leaders do not realize they were this close to the iceberg. "This is just normal, given how challenging things are. It's fine; keep going," they tell themselves. But it's not fine. These are signs that you are moving on the continuum of mental health toward the not-so-good end. You can't override your health.

Anxiety

We sometimes hear the word "anxiety" to mean the stress and nervousness we experience in normal life situations that represent a challenge, like before an important meeting or event. These are normal, temporary reactions. However, sometimes the signs are more persistent and intense and may involve, for example, worrying and feeling nervous; physical signs such as trembling, shortness of breath, and rapid heartbeat; and behaviors such as avoiding anxiety-generating situations.

At a high level, anxiety can often be conceptualized as a tendency for the brain to overestimate danger, make catastrophic predictions, and underestimate our ability to cope and the resources we have access to. Some have a predisposition, and most of us, given enough demands, will experience some level of anxiety. What I often see in professionals and leaders is a tendency to ignore the signs as they progress toward more frequency and more intensity, only paying attention when the level of anxiety reaches a point where it interferes with their functioning (for example, a panic attack at the airport or during a meeting). They then enter a cycle of avoidance, which often maintains, and at times entrenches, the problem.

Maybe you have experienced this, and if you have, you're certainly not alone. I often tell my clients that if I could get the people I work with together, they would see how similar their experiences are.

We will discuss cognitive behavior strategies in the next chapter, and the self-management techniques I mention there will contribute to increasing your baseline and serve as protective factors. The main thing to keep in mind, as it relates particularly to anxiety, is this: Be self-aware and pay attention to early signs. As early as possible, "manage your brain" to keep your thinking realistic. For example, remind yourself to distinguish between possibility and probability: "There is a possibility that I will forget an important part of my presentation, but the probability is low, and even if it does happen, it is not the end of the world." (You might think it is, but really, it isn't.)

Additional approaches to consider may include managing demands (for example, prioritizing) and managing boundaries (for example, saying "No" or saying "I will get back to you on whether I can add this to my list"), both at work and between work and your personal life. There will be times when "managing your brain" on your own will be easy; there may be other times when it will be very challenging. These are times when connecting with a resource such as a registered mental health professional might help.

Burnout

Sometimes people wonder why one would want to look at individual resilience, as this book does, since burnout is often caused by work-specific problems. The analogy sometimes used is that of a canary in a coal mine—we would not want to simply make the canary tougher.

I both love this analogy and don't love it. I love it because it clearly reminds us that burnout is not an individual issue, but instead a problem in the relationship between work and the individual, sometimes with the entire source of the problem being work. What I do not love about this analogy is that we are not birds. We have agency, and we need to have our own health in order to manage the situations we face. We need to see burnout for what it is: an occupational phenomenon; a systemic organizational problem that sometimes includes poor working conditions and other factors. Yet the individual cannot just wait for these to change. We need to act, and in order to take any action, we need to be as psychologically healthy as possible.

Burnout is an occupational phenomenon. It involves an occupational environment and a person, and it can be conceptualized as a relationship breakdown, often emerging gradually. Burnout is often not just within a person, or an individual problem. It can lead to a variety of physical conditions and psychological health conditions (such as depression), but burnout is not a diagnosis.

Burnout, as defined by the World Health Organization, requires three components: exhaustion, cynicism, and decreased performance. Exhaustion is often a result of unmanageable demands and inadequate recovery. Cynicism is often a result of a value conflict, disrespect, or emotional distance that has set in. And decreased performance is often related to lack of recognition, impossible standards, and a lack of control. When experiencing all three at once, most see an impact on their physical and mental health. Burnout has been associated with cardiovascular disease, high body mass index, high cholesterol, insomnia, depression, and other health issues. Depression is the largest and fastest-growing category of mental health disability claims in North America and Europe.

Most industries globally have seen their rates of burnout increase during the COVID-19 pandemic. Much research, including a study by Dr. Victor Dzau and his colleagues, has shown that a high number of professionals were reportedly suffering from burnout prior to the pandemic. The numbers across many industries have since increased. Nurses, for example, have been reported to reach rates of burnout of 60 percent, twice the generally reported average.

Anyone in any role can suffer from burnout. Burnout is a risk of all occupations. Compassion fatigue can arise when an additional source of demand occurs as a result of chronic use of empathy when working with other people's pain. Compassion fatigue has historically been associated with caring roles such as those in health care and education. With COVID-19 and its far-reaching implications, people across all industries experienced compassion fatigue, and particularly those in leadership roles, both formal and informal. As leaders and coworkers go through more significant challenges and look to support each other better, one implication is that compassion fatigue can now affect most lines of work.

Compassion fatigue is one of the ways one may get exhausted; it constitutes materially significant additional demands. Compassion fatigue is specific to the emotions inherent to the work we do if our work involves compassion for others. It tends to accumulate over time. It is there whether you want it, recognize it, or try to ignore it. And it boosts one of the key variables in the burnout equation, exhaustion, because it demands energy.

All three components of burnout can involve both workplace and personal contexts. None of them must happen, but all of them *can* happen, and there are actions we can take to reduce risk. Even if we conceptualize burnout as a relationship breakup, we want to look at what we as individuals do have control over.

Your Price Is Higher Than Your Employer's Price

There is another reason we have to lead our resilience from an individual perspective even if burnout is an occupational phenomenon. The two partners, you and your workplace, are not equal. The price for you as an individual is much higher than the price for your workplace. And as individuals, it is important that we keep this in mind. On the one hand, even if each burnout and potential work absence affects the workplace, the workplace has other resources; it is diversified, supported by many teams and individuals. You, on the other hand, the individual, don't have a multi-disciplinary

You don't have a
multi-disciplinary
team paid to
support you—you
only have your
own health.

———————

team paid every day to support you, and you only have your own health, not an infinite number of other "lives" you can use and start fresh from in case this one slides down. It will be all on you. That realization often comes with a disillusionment that is healthy and realistic.

Many work cultures convey the belief that professionals and leaders are somehow immune to stress, and as professionals they should be able to manage whatever stress they experience. They should feel so little distress that they have little need for recovery. Or they should not feel any distress, so there's no need for recovery.

Cultures do change, typically gradually. However, for now, what is more likely to resonate is the risks for professionals and leaders if they become burned out—risks for the quality of their work, and the risk of professional errors. Some may consider the risk of burnout an ethical imperative—a duty for professionals to know that there is a substantial likelihood that their competence is impaired and that they must manage the situation.

You may be wondering, "Am I currently experiencing a manageable level of stress, or is it burnout?" Ultimately a conversation with a health professional will help you answer this question, but at a high level, you are looking at frequency and severity. With regards to exhaustion, if you feel exhausted once, it's probably okay—it means you have an interesting life, and you can recover. If your exhaustion is constant, however, that is different. With regards to cynicism, if most conversations you have involve you complaining, and you are losing love for what you do, it could be a sign of burn-out. Usually, the longer you are on a job, the better you are at it, but if longer starts meaning you feel more stuck, that's different.

There are a few misconceptions associated with burnout. First, unless you've seen the statistics across industries that show an average rate of burnout among workers of 30 percent prior to the COVID-19 pandemic—and, for some, rates pushing 50 to 60 percent in the years following—you may not realize how prevalent it is. Second, we often hear people assume that feeling tired, overextended, and exhausted is the same as burnout. It is just one component. Sometimes it is a precursor to the full phenomenon, so it's worth paying attention to, but it's not burnout. A study by Dr. Christina Maslach and Dr. Michael Leiter has shown that disengagement (or cynicism), the second factor, was potentially a better proxy for burnout than exhaustion. This is changing, but many still assume that burnout is caused by individual weakness, which we know is not the case. Thinking that burnout only affects the individual is unrealistic and incomplete. Third, until you've been exposed to burnout yourself, you may believe that if you push through you can keep going. Again, not true.

What is key is to watch for all three signs. You want to notice them early, even when they are at a 2 on a 0-to-10 scale. In the early stages, we feel overextended, disengaged, ineffective. And in initial stages, we know from research that it starts with one of the three. One study led by Dr. Michael Leiter done before the pandemic with more than 1,700 health care employees, including a wide range of clinical, administrative, and support areas (with nursing being the largest group), showed this: 44 percent were engaged and experienced none of the three signs, and 56 percent had signs. Within this group, 11 percent were overextended, 7 percent were disengaged, and 30 percent felt ineffective; and 8 percent had all three signs, so were burned out. These numbers are very consistent across various health care roles and studies.

We want to keep in mind that public health emergencies, like a pandemic, or other events, like disasters or violence, impose additional demands on all of us, even if at different degrees. You may live in a culture that values putting work or others before yourself. It is important that you keep in mind the demands of emergencies and disasters.

The relationship between work and the individual may become strained due to all kinds of external circumstances, potentially leading to burnout. Research also points to individual risk factors, which include the following:

- Being in an early career stage, often because individuals at the beginning of their career have positive bias (in other words, they tend to judge reality favorably), feel the most stressed, and are most likely to disregard it

- Being low on self-care, for whatever reason

- Previous experiences of burnout

- Being stressed, fatigued, or psychologically distressed due to other stressors

Workplace stressors include challenges with organizational or leadership support, regulatory concerns, insufficient variety in caseload, and ethical violations. Personal-life stressors include bereavement, moving, changes in marital status, and financial challenges.

These factors are important because, even if this is about the relationship between work and an individual, and even if some of the responsibility (sometimes most) may be with the workplace, ultimately the human who will suffer is you, the individual. Taking individual leadership in managing this is key. Some cultures are a key contributor. The point is that burnout is not inevitable, but we need to take an active role.

One of my clients early on was a university student in a highly competitive program. Sam had a high volume of classes, all with weekly deliverables, and he had a math class that had only a mid-term and a final. This was a pattern he'd had the previous term, and it had not gone well. He knew he should work on the math class, but the short-term demands and deliverables of the other classes meant he could not bring himself to put time in on it. Sam was, as most of us would be, struggling with the psychological distance between now and the mid-term and final. What we did was calculate the number of hours he needed realistically to put in to succeed in the two math tests, which clearly pointed to the weekly number of hours he needed to spend on that class. We paired this with a weekly record of time he put in and what he accomplished. This decreased the psychological distance for him.

You also need to decrease the psychological distance between the context you currently operate in and the impact it might have on your mental health in the moderate term. Your context may not provide a protective structure today, but you need one, and you need to create it. The plan you'll implement today needs to come from you internally if it's not coming from an external source.

As you improve your resilience by restoring your supply-demands ratio, you decrease your risk on the first factor of burnout, exhaustion. A study by Dr. Fiona Yu and her colleagues has shown that when nurses experience high job demands, they perceive resilience as a protector and buffer against developing burnout. There is a limit to this, of course—jobs can become tougher, and if building resilience just allows you to push one notch harder, then you are undoing the benefits of additional resilience. Also, in such cases, resilience increases your personal resources but not your work resources.

How will you know if you're heading toward burnout or compassion fatigue? First, watch for any signs of your resilience going down. The early warning signs of burnout and compassion fatigue tend to be similar to those associated with a loss of resilience and other challenges, and include, for example, consistent and significant problems sleeping, concentration problems, difficulty making decisions, feeling nothing, and turning to alcohol to cope.

As things remain chronic, you may start seeing these responses and symptoms. On the behavioral side, you may see hypervigilance and startled reactions. On the cognitive side, you may see memory loss, difficulties with calculations, and reduced attention span. Physically, you may experience fatigue, nausea, digestive system problems, and heart palpitations. You may also notice misattributions of normal arousal; for example, hyper-suggestibility, including from rumors and false information, and interpretation of normal physiological arousal as serious illness. You may also notice relationship problems—at work or with your friends or family. Further down the road, you may see the following signs (by then, the recommendation is to connect with a professional):

- phobic avoidance of reminders
- out-of-the-ordinary level of grief
- frequent episodes of intense anger
- severe sleep disruption or frequent nightmares
- severe and ongoing anxiety
- clinical depression
- significantly impaired problem-solving
- distressing intrusive thoughts

We want to focus on both sides of the individual-work relationship, and as proactively as possible. We need to keep in mind that it is not an equal relationship. Ultimately, the individual pays a higher price.

Your Next Action (2 minutes)

If someone in your life, whether professional or personal, calls you their "rock," consider having a conversation about alternatives and why it may be healthier for all if you do not maintain this unhelpful and unrealistic role.

Questions for Reflection

- Have you been called a rock? How did that make you feel?
- Who is part of your support system?
- What are your early signs of decreasing resilience?

Remember

- There are benefits in challenging your assumptions about workplace mental health and increasing your awareness of the continuum of resilience and psychological health as a professional and leader.

- Professionals and leaders can find themselves on the path to burnout, anxiety, and workplace mental health disability absences.

- Be self-aware and pay attention to early signs of a decrease in your resilience.

- If you're anxious, think about what is possible versus probable. (Possibly you'll forget your presentation. But *probably* you will not.)

- There are three components to burnout: exhaustion, cynicism, and decreased performance. Burnout is a risk of all occupations.

- By spending time with this book, you have already become better equipped to realistically assess and take action on both your own risk and that of others.

—[3]—

Cognitive Behavior Management for Tapped-Out Professionals and Leaders

---

After two years of delivering virtual keynotes and workshops, I finally returned to live events. I loved being back, speaking in person, and it was going very well. Fabulous, in fact. I was nailing it.

Then it happened—the thing all speakers dread.

The night before one of my talks, I don't sleep well. Since I'm always absolutely prepared for my presentations, I tell myself it's fine and to shake it off. I can handle a little sleep deprivation.

At the venue, I meet the event team. They are all dressed in black, and they are fantastic. One person is on their laptop. Another is on the camera. One is standing at the door, wearing an earpiece. Others move about the room setting things up, making sure I have everything I need.

This event is what we call "produced"—it's a big stage, with two big screens, and monitors in front of the stage that show me my slides and my time.

When it's my turn to speak, I am introduced, and as I step on stage, the song "Back in Black" by AC/DC is playing. Love that song, but it's a little surprising. I go with it.

A few minutes into my talk, everything is going well and the audience is with me, which I love. Then I catch myself in the monitors—it's me in reverse. I can't stop looking at my movements. *Too much hands! Don't move around so much!* I try to tell myself to let it go, to stay focused. It gets really crowded in my brain, really fast.

That's when it happens. I blank. Completely. I can't remember what comes next.

I search my brain, trying to remember what I last said—nothing. The audience is silent. I look out at them, hoping to jog my memory—nothing.

Come on, MH.

In the audience, a woman bursts into nervous laughter. Maybe she thinks it's staged.

No matter what I try, I can't remember what comes next in my talk. It goes on forever. The man in front of me grows a beard, and the woman next to him retires. Ten thousand years pass and I am still up here trying to remember my line. *What is going on? What am I going to do to get out of this?*

Finally, my memory kicks in, and I know the next point of my talk. I keep going. Just like that, time speeds up again, and I'm back in the zone.

I get to the end of my speech. The audience loves it. They have takeaways. It's a great success.

So what happened? How did I remember my talk and deliver a good speech?

I fell back on my training—all my training—and how it shaped both my thoughts and my behaviors. As a speaker, I used my rehearsal process when I forgot my lines and then figured out my way through, telling myself, "I've got this." I used my training as a doctor in psychology and researcher, telling myself, "They want me to keep going. They are rooting for me."

I had practiced starting the talk from anywhere in case of unplanned interruptions, so moving forward had a familiar muscle memory. That's in part how we create a coping mechanism. I also took a deep breath and refocused on why I was there and why I'd brought my message, and all went well after that.

It felt like many long minutes, but it lasted just a few seconds.

In both my work as a psychologist and my roles as a senior leader, I've worked with lots of people. In recent years, I have had the chance to be retained by very accomplished individuals, just like you. They come to me either because they are experiencing challenges or because they are actually doing very well and want to optimize their situation.

What I discovered is that part of the problem—or part of what is keeping them away from a solution or a more optimal experience—is their thinking.

In business, we say that culture eats strategy for breakfast. In resilience, unhelpful thoughts eat your best intentions for breakfast. So we need to manage them first.

Keeping in mind that challenges can be external, you're still the one who will have to deal with them, manage them, or leave. Therefore, you'll need to make your own resilience and mental health as strong as possible today, and that starts with how you think.

Cognitive Biases

We often think of roadblocks as external to us. What we miss is how much we could manage one thing we do have control over that would likely change our experience significantly: our thoughts. Not only do we not optimize our thoughts— sometimes we make things worse.

Your cognitive biases are not always negative, and they are not your fault. This is just how our brains work. And you cannot choose how your brain works, but you can choose— you must choose—to know your mind as much as you can and optimize how you manage it. Which we don't always do.

As a speaker, I spend many days in airports. I'm a regular at those stores that sell magazines, books, and expensive candy bars. A few years ago, I was standing in the book section at an international airport, looking for my next read, when I saw a kids' book that would be great for my son, Alex, who had just turned five.

Alex was struggling to understand why I had to be gone so much, and this book was written just for him to explain what Mommy does when she's away. The only problem was that the book was called *When Daddy Travels*. Great. Did it not occur to the author that perhaps there might be a mother out there who does the traveling?

I was pretty ticked off. *Just one more example of what's wrong in the world,* I thought. *Just another illustration of inequality. And what about lesbian couples with children—what do they do? I am not going to send this message to my child; no way.* As I walked away, I muttered to myself, "*Je ne peux pas croire qu'on en est encore là; franchement, c'est incroyable!*" ("I can't believe we're still there; really, it's unbelievable!")

After I had a chance to calm down, I realized that maybe the book was better than nothing. I thought, *What's most important at the moment: Is it equality or is it to help Alex understand what I do, and can I convey the equality message in other ways?*

The next week, when I went through that same airport, I couldn't find the book. I asked a person on staff if they still had a copy of the book.

"Unfortunately, we ran out," they said. "But we have *When Mommy Travels.*"

"Oh, is it new?" I asked.

"No. We've had it for a few weeks."

Turns out that the book had been there all along. I'd just assumed it wasn't. And I'd let my assumptions create my reality and acted on those assumptions without testing them against reality. I had not asked the first time, had not looked around, had not looked online. I'd just run with my initial interpretation. We need to listen to our self-talk and watch for possible biases in order to make good decisions. This is true for both our work and our personal lives. Quite often, we go way beyond the facts, which is not helpful.

I see this in the workplace very often. Two different personalities do not check their assumptions, and this becomes a conflict. Or a junior professional assumes the more senior knows best, does not raise their question, and finds out later that they would have been right and an error could have been avoided.

Cognitive Strategies: Your Thoughts

In psychology, we have a very well-established, powerful model that has repeatedly, for decades and thousands of studies, showed its efficacy in helping people with treatment for depression, anxiety disorders, and countless other psychological disorders. This type of psychological treatment, a form of talk therapy, typically brings people who are clinically depressed—so depressed they cannot leave the house and go to work—out of clinical range within twelve weeks. You don't have to have a diagnosis and be psychologically ill to benefit from it.

If we bring these tools and use them proactively while we are in what we call a functioning range—a high-functioning range, even—then we have a chance of being high functioning even more often and of protecting ourselves from moments when we could slide toward a point where we're not functioning well. And to do this, we very much need to see our resilience and mental health on a continuum.

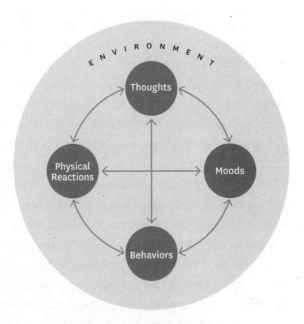

Five-part model to understand life experiences.

COPYRIGHT 1986 BY CHRISTINE A. PADESKY.

This model is called cognitive behavior therapy, or CBT. If you are interested in diving into this in a practical way, one of the best books on this topic, and the one I recommend to my clients and audiences, is *Mind Over Mood* by Dr. Dennis Greenberger and Dr. Christine A. Padesky. CBT basically refers to the fact that, as humans, we have thoughts, feelings, and behaviors all related to each other, and usually that all works out—but sometimes it doesn't.

For example, today you may have felt inspired and energized and thought, "Great, let's see what I can incorporate into my life from this fabulous book!" Sometimes, however, it doesn't work out so well. On other days, your thinking may be, "I'm not going to change anything in my life because of this book," and you may feel discouraged. Different thoughts and feelings; same book. Right now, some readers may be thinking, "Damn, she's amazing. I have to book her for our next event!" Others may be thinking completely different thoughts.

So it starts with the thoughts, which we call "automatic thoughts" because they come very fast. One of the things we know happens when we're having difficult feelings is that these thoughts tend to have two characteristics. One is that they tend to be negative; of course, nothing surprising there. But the second one is more important: They tend to be a bit *biased*. That means they're more negative than they need to be. And because the link between our thoughts and our feelings is a direct one, we're going to feel worse than we need to feel, and we're going to behave worse than we want to behave, and that's going to modify how we think—and now we're spiraling down.

The key problem here is that we buy into our thoughts as if they're a reality, as if they're facts. And, therefore, they shape how we feel and how we behave. That's when we're at risk of spiraling down. Instead, what we want is to view our thoughts as hypotheses to be confirmed, or not, by evidence. If evidence does not support them, then we want to change our thoughts into more realistic, fairer thoughts. We're not at the mercy of our thoughts.

For example, you may think, "This is impossible; there is no solution to this," which may lead you to feel discouraged and stop looking for options. However, the reality is that solutions do not always appear when and how we want them; sometimes we need to connect with others or with additional resources. Plus, we can't predict the future—you may identify a solution next week. Just thinking that "there is no solution to this" does not make it true.

That knowledge is important because viewing your thoughts as hypotheses is something that's in your hands. If you apply this approach, your brain will work better, and it gives you more control over something in a context where there are so many things you can't control. It gives you the ability to steer your own ship, so to speak.

What may help, therefore, is to catch your thoughts and change them into more realistic thoughts. Now, you may be thinking, "Yeah, yeah, I know that, and it makes sense, but it does not work for me. Even if I know that what I think is not realistic and I'm aware of what is more logical, I still feel anxious." There are reasons for this and ways to change it. You wouldn't go to physio for treatment of an injury and say to your physiotherapist, "Yes, I understand the exercise, but I don't need to do it."

Part of the mistake here is that even if you have some rational thinking about whatever your situation is, such as,

"I know they won't really fire me," you still have your automatic thoughts that say, "Everyone thinks I'm incompetent and I'll get fired," so your anxiety will stay. You need to manage your thoughts related to "Everyone thinks I'm incompetent" and actively change it to, "I can't read minds, and I have evidence of having contributed."

The misconception is that the ability to think rationally should fix the problem, but because it doesn't, you think managing your thoughts doesn't work, when in fact you have not optimized or even done the work. You wouldn't tell your physiotherapist that the exercises they've asked you to do don't work if you have not really done them.

What we want to do with negative and biased automatic thoughts is 1) realize they are there, and 2) change them to realistic thoughts. The more you know about how you tend to bias your thoughts, the easier it gets. There are categories for the ways most of us bias and distort our thinking. Here are the four that my clients seem to face most often, and they form the acronym BEAR:

B is for black-and-white, or all-or-nothing, thinking; e.g., "There is nothing I can do."

E is for emotional reasoning; e.g., "I feel like an impostor, so I am."

A is for anchoring; e.g., "I've always been fine and will continue to be."

R is for reading people's minds; e.g., "They all think I can't do anything right."

In resilience, unhelpful thoughts eat your best intentions for breakfast.

———————

What we need to do is turn the automatic thought into a more realistic thought. We do this by questioning the thought, much the same way a judge would if we were in court. For example, if the original thought is, "I can't handle one more change," we might ask, "What evidence do I have of this, and what evidence do I have of the contrary? If I asked others, what would they say?" And then turn the thought to a more realistic one. Perhaps, "I have gone through many changes, and I wish it would slow down, but I can likely go through this one, one step at a time."

Think of a specific time, let's say at work, recently, when you found yourself having a negative feeling. Now, as if you were watching a movie, pinpoint one of the most difficult moments, hit pause on the "movie," and write down one of the immediate, automatic thoughts you had in that moment. Remember, this is going to be negative and biased; something like, "No one values my work," or, "I can't change anything." It can also be a thought you've heard someone say to you.

When I ask leaders to do this exercise in my trainings, I often get the response, "No one is interested in my ideas." Many of us have had this automatic thought at one point or another. It can cause us to feel discouraged or even worthless, and it likely leads to us not saying a word.

Just telling yourself, "Okay, it's probably not true," is not going to change the feeling. You need to change the thought itself. And to do this, you need to get a bit granular. If you challenged this thought, you would ask yourself, "Am I

100 percent certain that no one is interested in my ideas? No, my colleague in the other team, each time we chat, seems to be interested, just like I am in her ideas. Maybe my leader here is not specifically commenting positively on my recent couple of contributions, but it does not mean no one is interested in my ideas."

Something more realistic, something a judge would let you say, may be more along the lines of, "Some people, like my colleague Maryna, are interested in my ideas, and I can't read my leader's mind," which then may make you feel a bit supported, a bit encouraged, and maybe curious about how to connect even better with even more members of the team, or at least to let go of their opinion. And as a result, you are more likely to speak up, often at each meeting.

Sometimes people ask me, "Is it just me?" and, "Am I the only one thinking this way?" Here we have this whole pile of cognitive distortions. Almost everyone thinks this way. Automatic thoughts are like bears in Canada.

Imagine you're camping in Canada in the summer, at a lake, in the mountains. You know you are in bear country. You may not have seen one yet, but you know they are around. You're not behaving as if there were no bears, as if they did not exist. And if you see one, you won't say, "What's a bear doing here?!" You know that you have the responsibility to manage this relationship both for the bear and for you, whether with structures, like bear-safe garbage bins, or behaviors, like storing food away from your tent. And you're clear on one rule: Don't feed the bears.

Cognitive distortions function the same way. Our brain is bound to make them at times, and unless we take certain actions, our brain will run away with these thoughts, which may have consequences. At times this may not be problematic—or it could be quite costly or severe. Instead of wishing or pretending they are not there, the better approach is to take the responsibility to get to know our mind as much as we can to navigate with it. We don't want to nourish thought processes that don't work well for us—we don't want to "feed the bears."

But we can live with them. So the same thing applies here: We're going to have these thoughts, but we don't want to feed them. We want to be able to realize we have them, catch them, and then change them to realistic thoughts.

This is easier said than done. What is fascinating here is that no matter the amount of knowledge or solid, research-based information you have, unless you implement strategies now and maintain them in tough times, you may still encounter these bears.

The three categories of interventions you will want to maintain, especially in tough times, are cognitive (focused on thoughts), behavioral (actions you'll take), and structural (actions in the workplace). The cognitive strategy I've introduced so far is called cognitive restructuring. You're changing—restructuring—your thinking. There are other ways to do this, but challenging the thought through Socratic questioning is a good place to start.

Behavioral Strategies: Your Actions

One of the easiest ways to prevent cognitive biases and distortions wherever we can isn't to catch and change them; that is quite a bit of work. It is to avoid them altogether. It's like camping in an RV and putting all your food in it, door closed. If we set things up in such a way that our brain will go in the right direction, the bears will not even show up and we'll react the way we were hoping to. A way to do that is to design and implement rules that will protect us from our unhelpful thinking. Behavioral economics calls this choice architecture.

The behavioral approach is the most powerful. You are basically creating a structure, rules, roles, and ways things will be done no matter what. Specifically, *no matter what you think*. A great example of this approach is to have standard checklists. For example, the Canadian Psychological Association has a ten-step guideline for an ethical decision-making process. If you think you have an ethical issue, you take out your sheet with the ten steps and apply that lens.

Still on the behavioral side, there are actions you could implement related to lifestyle. This is key: In my experience, what wears down high-functioning individuals is not the challenges they are asked to solve in their actual work—they are great at this—but the lack of systematic recharging, which then puts them at risk of having thoughts that are unhelpful or unrealistic. The top three actions to pay attention to are your amount of physical activity, nutrition, and sleep.

The main challenge with these lifestyle choices is not in knowing, but in doing. These are all research-based strategies, solidly established, that we know affect how the brain works, as they are core elements of "supply" in the supply-demands equation, so they deserve your commitment; they are not optional. They are the equipment you need to manage the bears.

Structural Strategies: Workplace Actions

The cognitive and behavioral approaches translate very well in the workplace. One strategy at work may be to identify where most mistakes are made, because unhelpful thinking is often part of the equation. Then, build a process to protect against it, instead of reminding team members to not make mistakes. For example, radiologists decrease their error rates by having checklists to use, which protects them against their own biases.

Another strategy is changing the beliefs that come from the culture you've been operating in. It could be the culture of your profession, which says things like, "You're a doctor; you're not the patient," or it could be the culture of an employer that says, "You have to be strong at all times," or, "You have to have the right answer all the time." These beliefs get in our head, and they represent the dominant discourse that's around us and that we practically integrate. But sometimes these beliefs are not helpful.

Recognize the effects of your profession's dominant discourse, put these beliefs to the test, see if they are realistic for you, and change them if they're not, if possible. The statements above could become something like, "I am a doctor, but I am also a human, and at times I need to be a patient," or, "My role requires me to convey strength, but as a human, at times I may not feel strong," or, "I work to have the best answers all the time, knowing that at times I won't, because no one does all the time."

Embracing Self-Management

By leading our own thinking, we're making sure that we untangle our thoughts early and align our feelings and behaviors. Even better, we're protecting ourselves from not doing so well. And if you find this is challenging, then do what you would do in any other area of your life: get professional help, like a psychologist or other regulated mental health professional.

The key is to take action. The following are examples of self-management techniques that can contribute to increasing your baseline and serve as protective factors:

- Physical activity (e.g., cardio, strength training, meditative activity such as yoga or meditation)
- Nutrition
- Sleep

- Relationships
- Volunteer work
- Time in nature
- Spirituality
- Pleasurable activities (e.g., writing, visiting art galleries, playing a musical instrument)
- Boundaries
- Reducing alcohol consumption or maintaining abstinence from alcohol

You may have to experiment to find out what works for you and have it on your radar every day, just as you would with physiotherapy exercises. See this as physiotherapy for your brain. With this, you are really doing self-management. And my recommendation is that you carve out daily time—not long; a few minutes will do—to make space to self-manage.

Resilience and burnout are related, but not 100 percent. The actions we take as individuals can partially act as a protective factor, but if we conceptualize burnout as a relationship, then part of the responsibility is in the workplace. Another part is in your own hands.

Daily Resilience Workout

Both in the literature on resilience and in my work, two themes are consistent: *awareness* and *actions*. Most people

I have worked with have agreed that implementing more awareness and actions would be helpful, but doing so just falls off their radar until a few days prior to their appointment with me. Some days I understand the piano teacher who can tell her students have not practiced.

The Daily Resilience Planner is a practice I have designed for my clients—one of them called it his "resilience workout," a phrase that is very fitting. It involves thirty seconds at the beginning of the workday and thirty seconds at the end. The first thirty seconds involves one task: You identify one or two actions you'll take today for your resilience and when you'll do them. The second thirty seconds involves two tasks: You identify what you did, as well as one resilience win and one or two resilience learning moments from today. You can find the Daily Resilience Planner in Appendix A.

Here are the reasons why this appears to work. First, you need to plan, otherwise it's very unlikely actions will just happen. Second, you need to recognize success (not just what did not work) and learn, which puts you in a growth mindset, and which we know from research is key to resilience. For example, in your first thirty seconds, you may decide on these actions: 1) a two-minute meditation before touching lunch, and 2) a twenty-minute walk before coming home. In your second thirty seconds, you may reflect that a win was that you managed to set a two-minute alarm on your phone and sit and breathe for two minutes; and that a lesson was that, because at the end of the day you decided to look at your email one more time, ended up staying for fifteen more minutes, and missed your twenty-minute walk, you need to eject yourself on time to ensure you walk.

Some people customize this for themselves. For example, if you tend to disregard demands, maybe you also list one new demand that has emerged during the day, in addition to a win and lesson. For some, this is a motivator to protect resilience actions in a realistic way.

Everyone has sixty seconds. And most of my clients have chosen to do this in a little notebook on their desk. Not electronic, which for many is a slippery slope toward work. An additional step to this is to do a weekly one-minute review to flip through your notes and collect what become your own guidelines for resilience at the end of your notebook, which you would then read each week and, as this builds up, each month. It may look like this:

- End-of-week learning: When I consider my action a "rule" and just stop everything and do it, I manage to do it and it does not take away from my work time.

- End-of-month learning: When I do my daily planning, even on days I am not working, it keeps resilience on my radar in a much clearer way.

Our work affects us in positive and negative ways through our experiences. As you pay attention to yourself and your work situation, you'll contribute to having a burnout-informed organization, and you'll increase your visibility and the opportunity to alter your overall quality of life and professional resilience.

You may even do this with people around you at work and in your personal life. When it comes to managing your thoughts, don't do it because it makes sense or because your boss told you to, or even because I say you should. Do it because you have control over this, and that's in part what's going to make you more resilient.

What bears have shown up in your life? Are you feeding them or sending them away? Manage your thinking as a way to bring forward an even better version of yourself and to be more resilient. Just remember: Don't feed the bears.

Your Next Action (1 minute)

Experiment with the Daily Resilience Planner in Appendix A. With a focused, concrete structure to support your efforts, you have a better chance of being successful. This takes a total of one minute per day and has the potential to change your outlook, as you will experience either the satisfaction of accomplishment or the positive benefits of learning. Either way, you win.

Questions for Reflection

- What are your BEARS or the BEARS you see most often at work?

- What has been your experience with the Daily Resilience Planner? What have you noticed?

- If you have not tried it yet, what got in the way for you, and how can you overcome this?

Remember

- One thing we have control over is our thoughts. We need to listen to our self-talk and watch for possible biases to make good decisions.

- Cognitive behavior strategies have been shown to help.

- Our thoughts are not facts. Try to view thoughts as hypotheses to be confirmed, or not, by evidence.

- Avoid BEAR thinking.

- The top three behaviors to pay attention to are physical activity, nutrition, and sleep.

- If you find self-management difficult, then do what you'd do in business: Get professional help from a psychologist or other regulated mental health professional.

- Everyone has sixty seconds they can use to self-assess.

—[4]—

Supply, Demands, and You

When my son, Alex, was ten, I drove him and his friend Patrick home after school. They sat in the back seat, chatting and singing along to songs, completely ignoring that I was in the car. A few minutes into the drive, they were quiet.

Then Patrick said, "I have depression." *Okay*, I thought, *he's sharing something with Alex. Just listen.*

Then Alex said, "Oh, that sucks." Okay. That's in the supportive range for a ten-year-old.

I prepared to put on my psychologist-mom hat and gently join the conversation, but before I could say anything, Patrick said, "I'm good again."

Then Alex asked, "You started seeing friends again?"

That's an odd expression for a child, I thought.

Patrick said, "Yes, and I changed jobs."

Changed jobs?

As it turned out, Alex and Patrick were playing a game on their phones, a game in which you gain or lose points as you progress through life events. It feels that way sometimes, doesn't it? That we lose or gain points as we deal with the demands of life?

You may have played similar games. The board game Life—where you get a little car and spin the wheel to find out if you get more education, commit to a relationship, spend time with friends, have children, pick up a pet, buy a house— features the decisions you may make as you progress through life. You win or lose based on the impact of those decisions— those moves.

The game Alex and Patrick were playing on their phones was different. It did one thing Life and other games like it don't do: It considered the impact of these demands, these decisions, and these moves on the player's mental health. In the game, Patrick's avatar had stopped seeing his friends. His job wasn't going well. And so he started losing points and became depressed.

The game provided real-time, clear, realistic feedback to Patrick on the impact of his context on his mental health. And because he had this feedback, he could easily course correct, make the necessary moves to optimize his situation, and start winning again. Over time, his avatar could become more resilient, because Patrick gained a better understanding of what would cause him to "lose points."

In real life, if we wait until we're affected, we are left with reactive approaches to anxiety, compassion fatigue, and burnout. We act after we've experienced a fair bit of psychological pain, and the climb back to health can be long. That said, we do have very effective treatments in psychology and pharmacology to help, sometimes combining both. But they take time.

If instead we have a leadership approach to actions that an individual and a workplace can take to decrease the risk of anxiety, compassion fatigue, and burnout, then we have a chance of influencing the outcomes. Taking a proactive role does not take a lot of time. Just reading this chapter will likely decrease your own risk, and it can save you a lot of time.

Particularly if you have chosen your line of work because it means something important to you and is aligned with what you value, you care. You may care about the people you help and work with; you may care about the integrity of your work, your brand as a professional, or the quality of your financial analyses, for example. Most roles also require that you use your full self, including your emotions, to do a good job. This often includes leadership and helping roles. We know from research, and I know from working with many, that work that is value-driven can put you at increased risk of burnout. If you didn't care, it would not affect you as much.

Expecting that anyone can work, particularly doing value-driven work, without being affected has been compared to wading through water and expecting not to get wet. The key, if I can add to this analogy, is to recognize you'll get wet and ensure you plan for and implement ways to dry. Drying may include stepping out of the water and being exposed to warmth and wind. If there is sun and wind but you stay in the water, you'll still be wet. If you step out of the water but it's raining, you'll still be wet. We are in an interrelated system within work and outside of work.

The Demands and Your Mental Health

Let's try an exercise. List three stressors you currently have at work. Now add as many additional stressors as you can, both at work and in your personal life. You have likely listed negative stressors. Add positive ones as well, the parts of your work and non-work contexts that represent demands on your energy even if they are positive and desired.

One blind spot I often see in my psychology practice is not realizing that the demands are both work and personal. (And this has been observed in research as well.) The other key blind spot is focusing only on the negatives.

I once worked with an exhausted client who did not know what was going on for her. She had all she wanted: a promotion at work with a supportive team, an upcoming wedding and trip, and a move to a dream house. She also had a constant stream of visitors, which meant she went out often. These demands were all positive, and most were not related to work, and yet they were exhausting her. As we worked to clarify her values and context, her strategic resilience plan included a pillar focused on managing her energy with actions like monitoring herself on a regular basis. Another pillar focused on boundaries, with actions like proposing alternate dates to friends and family when requests were not spaced enough to allow a return to her daily and weekly routines. I'll discuss this more in the next chapters.

As we build your custom mental health strategy, the framework we'll use will protect you from your own blind spots, ensuring that you factor in all the stressors and demands you are responding to.

We have to start with this for two reasons. Given the focus on work outcomes, sometimes we're unaware of what affects us and how, or if we're aware, we don't acknowledge it as valid and certainly don't share it with others. The reality is that if we're going to change that curve, we'll need to have compassion, both for ourselves and for our colleagues. They, and we, are not alone. Some of our demands are also experienced by others, and some of our reactions are also experienced by others. We are in a system, a relationship that we as individuals have with our workplace.

Report Accurately (to Yourself) on Your Sources of Supply and Demands

Heard from a leader: "Work is no busier now than before. No idea what's wrong with me."

The balance between optimism and realism can be complex. With the exception of lawyers, for whom realism is often adaptive, most professionals and leaders are more on the optimistic side and believe that they balance both. In my experience, many fall significantly more on the optimistic side, and that would include me. This mindset has several advantages. For example, entrepreneurs and intrapreneurs (those who start something within an organization) would often never start the things they do if they did not tip toward the optimistic side.

When it comes
to your resilience,
tipping too far
toward optimism
can become
a liability.

———————

When it comes to your resilience, tipping too far toward optimism can become a liability. As you assess and report (to yourself) on your particular resilience context, the tendency to overestimate your sources of supply and underestimate, or even completely miss, your sources of demands can leave you with a very reliably invalid assessment of where you stand. This in turn leads to an inaccurate perspective on the risks you're taking.

Lynn is the professional who told me, "Work is no busier now than before. No idea what's wrong with me." She values great work and has mostly had the chance to do just that in her career so far as an IT leader. As we started to assess her overall demands context, she mentioned that she had just been asked to cover for her boss's maternity leave, something she had done a couple of years prior. This came with a decrease of her other responsibilities, and she felt "very comfortable" with that.

"That's really it," she said. Even though she felt "comfortable" with her demands, they were still demands.

When I asked Lynn about the non-work part of her life, she mentioned that she had recently decided with her partner to get married—a positive demand, but still a demand. A good friend of hers whose family was out of the country had just been diagnosed with severe anxiety and was grieving her dad, so Lynn connected with her regularly. She loved her friend and wanted to do this for her, but it was still a demand.

As all this was going on, and for several reasons, Lynn had stopped some of her regular activities. "I've stopped exercising. I haven't connected with my friends, especially the people who are doing great. And the other day I realized it had been weeks since I had done anything for myself."

Lynn underestimated the demands at work and in her personal life and overestimated her supply, which minimized the necessity to prioritize and increase supply.

I want you to keep your optimism; I just want you to pair it with a more realistic perspective, which in the end allows you to take more effective actions. These actions will lead to positive outcomes, thereby feeding your self-efficacy, and further supporting optimism from a more realistic perspective, as Dr. Martin Seligman has found in his work.

Take an honest look at your sources of supply and demands. This exercise will likely require about fifteen minutes of your time at the most, but quite possibly three minutes.

First, start a list of your sources of supply. Sources of supply often represent protective factors, actions that we implement that increase our energy and health. The four most powerful ones we know of from research are physical activity (cardio, strength training, and meditative activity), nutrition, time with people we enjoy spending time with, and sleep. There are other areas. For example, you could increase your supply by protecting your boundaries, by spending time in nature, or by doing arts, if you enjoy that. It's important to know that even if you do these additional activities, the four most powerful activities have received the most empirical support. It does not mean that they are the only powerful supplies, but it does mean they are the ones research points to most consistently, so the associated return on investment is more likely.

Next, scan your daily, weekly, and monthly life over the past and next few months for anything that demands some of your energy. Look at both your work and personal contexts. At work, you may have a few difficult or challenging projects on your list, or you may be missing a team member or a colleague needs to be off work, so you need to cover for their absence. Or it could be in your personal life. Maybe your child is sick, your partner is in a career transition, your parents need more help, or good friends around you are moving or leaving a relationship. You may be managing a household, either concurrently with other things or exclusively right now, which could involve raising children, supporting a partner, and managing finances over which you have little control. And there are larger, at times chronic demands, like a pandemic. All these represent demands of your energy.

Example Sources of Supply and Demands

Professionals and leaders tend to fall into traps when I ask them to identify their sources of supply and demands. The main problem with assessing your supply is that you overestimate it just because you're feeling fine ("I'm feeling good, which means I've got a lot of supply and don't need to do more, plus I don't have time"). You also don't create buffers ("I'll have thirty minutes between these two meetings, so I'll go for a run"), and you don't create Plan Bs ("I don't have time to go for a run, so I'll skip exercise today"). This means that you may end up taking actions on the supply front that are easy to do, thinking this is sufficient ("I did eat salad on Monday, so I am good for this week"). These traps all lead to the outcome of not implementing the actions that would have increased your supply.

Sources of Supply	Sources of Demands
Physical health is good	Launching large project at work next month
Enjoy my work	
Relationship with partner is good	Business travel ramps up in the next three months
Time with my kids	Partner's health uncertain
Gym (rare these days)	Busy time of year at school for the kids
	Home maintenance weekly

On the demands side, you do the opposite. You underestimate the impact of the amount of demands you have. You say, "I can handle this too; bring it on," and the moment it's on your plate, you realize the impact. You also don't estimate well. You say, "This will take me fifteen minutes," and you're now two hours into the task and realize it can't be completed in one shot, and it will spread over a few days. You're acting as if you have more control over your demands than you do; they are in fact more numerous and larger than you thought, including new ones you had not accounted or buffered for.

And, therefore, it means you're creating even more imbalance between supply and demands. This overall approach is not working.

Think Like a Project Manager

You likely have had the chance to work with a project management professional. If you have not, this is something to look forward to. The project management professionals I have had the chance to collaborate with bring several strengths to any project. One of them is assessing the demands with a degree of realism and calm. When a project management professional is asked to add an item on the list, do they just say, "Yes, consider it done"? Probably not. They typically respond that they'll take it away and get back to you. Then, they come back with a picture of everything else that is already on the list, now with this new item, and turn to you to assess what else needs to move, given limited resources. There will be an unlimited number of demands coming your way, and you have a limited amount of supply. Seeing this clearly is critical.

For most leaders, this generates the conflicting reaction of both appreciation and impatience. They know they need to listen. This approach of realistically looking at as many aspects of your sources of supply and demands as you can ensures you don't get blindsided, whether by your own optimism or another not-so-helpful mechanism. It may also come in handy when considering the amount and types of demands you have been adding to your list. For your work on your custom personal resilience plan, you need to think like a project management professional.

One more note on the sources of supply and demands. Once they have their list, many people want to move to a clear recipe to assess what they see: "Should I have the same number on both sides?" and, "What if some weigh more than others?" and, "What does balance mean?" Try to see this information as one part of the equation for now. As we continue with the next steps, the direction you will want to take in designing your plan will get clearer. Jaana Rask, senior director of people and organization at Novo Nordisk in Switzerland, notes that leaders and professionals very much need a plan that isn't cookie cutter and static, and that such a plan is integral to a high-performance model. Clarity on your sources of supply and demands is key information for a customized and adaptable plan.

Nate is an accomplished professional and leader. He is a road cyclist and is naturally competitive in most things. He is the father of two daughters he loves. He is separated from his partner, in a co-parenting relationship that continues to be challenging, and he has a new relationship in his life, which is very positive.

As Nate wrote down his sources of supply and demands, he said, "Even just putting down the content for supply and demands opened my eyes and led to changes. I saw with new clarity where my time was going, and right there could see the misalignment with my values. I still had to put some time on some of these demands, but not as much as I was. For example, I can lower my goals for some of the chores, let go of a few, and maybe get help for one or two home-related demands, and instead enjoy more quality time with my partner and daughters. That in itself was transformational." Certainly, if, like Nate, you already see opportunities for adjustments, you can start taking action now.

So, what's your plan to reduce burnout risk in yourself and others? What will you do so you can protect your professional resilience, be engaged, and experience satisfaction and growth with your work?

If we were in Alex and Patrick's mobile game, how high would your professional resilience points be this week so far? How about today? What demands are on your radar, and how is your engagement and your effectiveness? Did you plan for recovery today? What did you learn from yesterday?

Your Next Action (10 minutes)

Go to the Supply/Demands Inventory in Appendix B (Activity Sheet 1): Decide on a timeframe (e.g., three months, one year) and write your realistic and observable sources of supply. Then, list the demands that are currently present and predictable over the timeframe. You'll need to define a clear timeframe to assess your demands accurately. Being realistic about what you list is critical for your plan. For now, spend about five minutes on each and write anything that comes to mind.

Questions for Reflection

- How do you feel about the supply side of your inventory?

- How do you feel about the demands side of your inventory?

- What would be your best realistic goal in the timeframe you have defined as it relates to supply and demands?

Remember

- While there seem to be infinite sources of demands and many options for supply, you are working with limited time resources. You are the one who gets to decide how you prioritize and which sources of supply and demands to focus on. You can be strategic about it.

- Many successful people feel particularly challenged by trying to change their personal habits, such as adding meditation or more regular physical activity. They feel like success should come more easily. Keep at it, daily.

- Start with clarity on your own supply and demands.

- There are situations where work and personal life demands are going to be impossible to match. Sometimes you'll need to put things on hold.

— [5]—

Your Values
and Context

The **professionals and leaders** I work with are so very competent in the technical part of their work that the contrast with finding effective solutions to deal with personal challenges, at work or at home, almost feels dissonant. They might say, "I have no idea why this is not easier for me to manage." My answer often involves a version of, "If it were that obvious and easy, we would all do this already."

As we look at what's going on, most leaders have popular and even research-based high-level information about what might help them. They then tell themselves they should try this; for example, they should exercise more. They manage to get out and exercise once over the course of a week (if that, and their plan was five times), and they continue to feel the same way. They conclude that it does not work, and they in fact feel worse both because the situation remains the same and now because they have not successfully implemented what they thought they should. This often generates a sense of failure, a territory that the professional and leader has worked hard not to visit often and does not like, to say the least. And so, they leave it promptly and return to working harder.

This is the proverbial opportunity. What is not working will often provide you with exactly what you need in terms of solutions, and this applies to your strategic resilience plan.

What's Your Goal?

Let's step back. A strategy involves identifying your goal; in this case, increasing your resilience. Within your strategy, we'll aim at identifying three key pillars—three main ways you're going to do this. And you'll identify actions within each of these pillars that you're going to take.

But it needs to be personalized. Even if a particular business can produce several products, it will typically focus on a few, often those most aligned with its mission and core expertise. Similarly, the goal of increasing your resilience needs to be aligned with you personally. It is not going to look the same for anyone else reading this book.

How do we personalize your plan? We tie it to your values—what is most important to you. Don't get hung up on the word "values." Some of what is most important to you may not be found on a list of typical values. It may include cooking, for example, or it could be something like power or learning. Include both professional and personal values for this first round. If in the future you want to explore each separately, that is also an option.

Take a moment and start filling out the Priority Values List, which is provided in Appendix B (Activity Sheet 2). You may need a bit more time across a few days. Clients I work with often confirm that letting their brain incubate this helps. For now, write some of what might be on that list for you, and write what is most important to you in life. No need to order them according to importance, and the list is for you only, so don't worry about a partner's reaction to what you put there. Start writing and try to get between three and ten values, at least; if you can, write more. Remember to use the definition of "values" broadly: just what is important to you in your life. Your list could include words like "generosity" and "creativity"; it may also include words like "mountains," "music," and "travel." If you need more time, you can add more later. Here's an example:

Example Priority Values List

Family

Health

Travel

Learning

Leadership

Now you have at least three. Given our end goal to create your strategic resilience plan, which means taking concrete action, we need to bring this list to life. The next step is to look at each of your values and start associating words of action with them. If you were to bring this specific value into your daily life, what would someone see you do, for example?

One of my clients, Jane, had generosity as a value, and one action was for her to volunteer her time to a charity. Jeff had cooking as something he valued, and one action was to try a new recipe regularly. Amy valued the outdoors, and an action she listed was taking a walk in the park close to her work. Note how she did not go straight to "going for a five-hour hike." This was probably part of her list, but versions of actions aligned with her value allowed her to creatively broaden ways to bring this value to her life daily. You may not have actions for every one of your values yet. Sometimes I don't know immediately and exactly how to translate a value into action, and that's okay. You'll create this list over time.

Which Values Will You Put on Hold?

Heard from a highly specialized professional audience member: "I like the idea of putting things in parentheses—on hold in a friendly way."

Here is the key to this part of the reflection: You're not going to be able to do everything in your strategic resilience plan because you have a full life. Resources are limited, just like in business. Which means you have to make choices. You're going to need to get clarity on what to focus on in the next little while—the next month, or six weeks, or whatever timeframe you choose. You'll also need to identify what you're going to put on hold, in parentheses. I know that I asked you a moment ago to list what is most important to you; we're not going to cut anything out. What we're doing is moving some to the forefront for now, with the others in parentheses. Think of it as "on hold" in a friendly way.

Resources
are limited, just
like in business.
Which means
you have to
make choices.

———————

On your list of values, which two or three would you focus on? Circle them. Which one could you put on hold for right now? Keep in mind that we are not ranking them, and no one's going to see your list, so you can change your mind later. You can even decide to shred these pages if you need. But for now, you need to connect your plan to your values. This is for your resilience, and if it helps, keep in mind that it will likely impact you and others positively.

Quadrants of Your Context

Chris was pregnant after three IVF attempts, she had just accepted a newly created and more senior role, one of her parents had health issues, and she and her partner had recently purchased their first home, which they loved. From her perspective, there were no major demands on her life; things were mostly "on track." Yet, sleep was sometimes an issue, and she wanted to make sure this would be optimized. I shared with her how, as an individual, looking at the four aspects of her personal context might give her the visibility she needed to ensure her optimism was paired with a dash of realism and allow her to approach her situation optimally.

Her perspective after the exercise was this: "I have high confidence and optimism as a person and generally tend to be on the resilient side. I can also be so optimistic and persistent that I disregard the reality of the demands I am facing, and that can be a risk because I then don't adjust my supply accordingly. My external context has many wonderful characteristics, including my husband, new home, stimulating and supportive job, great friends. It also has positive aspects that represent demands (which I had not thought of in that light), such as my promotion to this newly created role that I need to design as I go; my pregnancy; my mom's health, which does worry me; and this entirely new community we moved into, which is farther away from work and where I have everything to discover."

In business, strategic work requires, in part, having clarity on the context. You have likely recognized the structure of the business-based SWOT analysis (strengths and weaknesses in the internal business context, and opportunities and threats in the external context) in this example, where we identify what is helpful and not so helpful for this goal in our internal and external context.

Quadrants can translate to what is naturally present and either helping or creating a challenge in both our personal (internal) and external contexts. This rewording is important, because keeping a perspective that is both realistic and grounded in strength-based and self-efficacy perspectives is what we need to move forward.

Exploring these quadrants is part of what creates the path between where you want to go and how you can realistically get there, taking your own context into perspective. Do so by completing the Quadrants of Context exercise in Appendix B (Activity Sheet 3). Specifically, you want to collect information about what is naturally happening and helps toward your goal of increasing your resilience, and what may be contributing to challenges, both internally and externally. Starting with you as a person, internally, list what is naturally happening that helps, including your predispositions, your personality style, and your positive qualities. If nothing is coming to mind right now, finding this self-appreciation may be part of your goals, but for now, think of moments in your life when things were good. What were you naturally doing?

For example, let's say you get excited about ideas; it's just who you are naturally. Maybe something that helps is that you tend to be open-minded about change. That's easy for you. Or you like to cook healthy meals, or your motivation to take action on your personal resilience is high. All these would go in the quadrant of helpful personal context.

Then, list what are challenges you personally experience. Same approach: These include your predispositions, your personality style, and characteristics that may get in the way. Perhaps you tend to underestimate how long it will take you to do most things, you tend to say yes to most demands, your workday does not really end, or you tend not to protect time for self-care. Try to focus your content here as it relates to your resilience. For example, it's easy for me to go for a run; it's not easy for me to meditate.

The second part of this exercise is to do the same thing for your external context. What elements of your external context make supplying energy easy, and what elements make it not so easy to work toward increased resilience? Examples of aspects that may help include living in an area where you can walk out the door, or having found a yoga app that you like. Examples of aspects that may make things more challenging include having young children at home due to school closures, or having a role that feeds you a constant stream of demands that are right up your alley and you would love to meet but just cannot, given the hours available in your day.

Here's an example:

Example Quadrants of Context

	EASY	CHALLENGE
PERSONAL	Interested in many topics Good health even when I don't do much exercise	Take on too much Don't protect time for own health Don't protect time for family
EXTERNAL	Good work opportunities Supportive partner Good relationship with brother	Too many work demands Pressure to make more money

You now have the information and perspectives you need to create a strategic resilience plan that is yours and can realistically be implemented. As the components of these sections change and evolve, part of keeping the strategy alive will be to weave in the agility to update your analysis and modify the plan accordingly. It's the same in business; things will change, and we plan with what we know and can forecast to the best of our knowledge.

Your Next Action (10 minutes each)

Go to the Priority Values List and Quadrants of Context exercises in Appendix B (Activity Sheets 2 and 3):

1 List at least three values, or more if you can. Listing three to ten values focuses you on your own plan, not anyone else's. Next, circle the one to three that you'll focus on first (if you can, my recommendation is to pick only one to start), putting the others in parentheses for now. Doing so makes it easier to focus your plan. Then, for each of these values, list two to three concrete, observable actions that, if taken on any given day, would bring this value to life. That clarity will make it easier to outline actions within your plan. Start with ten minutes for this—it may be all you need.

2 List what characteristics of your personal internal and external contexts might help or represent challenges. This is critical to know, because they will affect your goals, and you can work with them in your plan only if you know what they are. Push yourself to write two or three items in each quadrant during a total of ten minutes. You can always add or revisit later.

Questions for Reflection

- What is most important for you in life?
- What key part of your context do you see now with more clarity?

Remember

- Start with clarity on your values and the forces affecting your context.

- Just as a business would consider its core competencies, core values, and context, this is often your best guide on the personal side as well.

- You have already made your Priority Values List. You are tapping into your values and using that lens to look at your supply and demands and inform your overall strategic resilience plan.

- Your plan must reflect your values.

- You can translate your values into actions; it requires extra thought, and it can start small. For example, "being outdoors" doesn't have to mean scheduling a five-hour hike. It can mean walking to work, going to the park on your lunch, or even just stepping outside for two minutes.

—[6]—

Design Your Strategic Resilience Plan

A s **Dr. Michael Porter**, Harvard Business School professor, wrote in a *Harvard Business Review* article, "The essence of strategy is choosing what not to do." Now that you have clarity about your Supply/Demands Inventory, your Priority Values List, and your Quadrants of Context, the next step is to identify your three strategic pillars. These represent the three main categories of actions you'll want to invest in to reach your resilience goal. If you find you have more, go ahead, but try not to have more than five. Three is just a reasonable number to start with.

Then, on the Custom Strategic Resilience Plan in Appendix B (Activity Sheet 4), identify the three categories of actions (pillars) you need to focus on to bring your priority values into your life even more, given the particular components of your context: sources of supply, sources of demands, and forces impacting your resilience goal.

When my client Marcus sat down to complete this next step, he had nothing to write. Because we had built the information about his particular values and context for the purpose of designing his custom plan, he pushed himself to put all that he had written in front of him. Then, he started looking at his selected values of balance and health and his context. He had challenges with a relentless technology start-up management role that felt like an endless demands-generating context. For him, this was paired with a habit of saying "yes," which was rapidly turning into an over-promise–under-deliver downward spiral. His strategic pillars became boundaries, self-care, and planning.

Marcus told himself, "Okay, I've written my values. I've looked at my supply and demands, and I know the importance of exercise, nutrition, and sleep, and I'm realizing that I'm really not protecting time with friends. It may be that one of my pillars is going to be relationships. I also realize I have way too many demands—I am there for others, but I don't have anyone in my corner, and I don't even know where to start. Well, maybe a strategic pillar will be to increase support around me. Maybe another will be focusing on myself more—self-care and connecting with someone to consult with regarding my work, like an executive coach."

Here are examples of pillars:

- Boundaries
- Self-care
- Commitment
- Simplicity
- Daring more often
- Relationships
- Mindfulness
- Recovery

Keep in mind that you may need or benefit from incubation, as most great ideas do. Incubation is a process often associated with creativity in which you let go of consciously focusing on the task at hand and go do other things. Your brain continues to work on it regardless, without any effort on your part. When you come back to the task, you might have additional perspectives and ideas, links that your brain made that your design will benefit from. What this means is that you might want to start the work on pillars, then leave it for a few days (during which incubation might take place). When you return to your plan, you'll probably find that you have more clarity and ideas.

Your Actions

The next step is to look at your strategic pillars and, for each pillar, identify two or three actions you can take that will bring the pillar to life. For example, if you listed increasing your sources of support, one action on the work side may be to connect with an executive coach; on the mental health side, it may be to connect with, say, a psychologist or other regulated mental health professional or your employee assistance program, so you can explore your own situation with a professional.

A critical aspect of this part of the process is that we want these actions to be absolutely doable in your context. This means they will likely need to be small: You could implement them today, given what's going on in your life, and maintain them for the next few months. They will likely seem insufficient to fully bring the strategic pillar to life, but that doesn't matter. We don't want an unrealistic plan that does not get implemented; we want a realistic plan that you start on today. Done is better than perfect, and when it comes to implementing changes and building self-efficacy, this is even more true.

A good test to assess if your actions are small enough is to ask yourself how certain you are that you'll implement it tomorrow, on a scale of 0 to 100 percent. Here is my rule: If that number is below 85 percent, then scale the action back until you are 85 percent certain or more you'll implement it. Note how we're not wondering if the action is small enough for *most people* to be able to do this. We're also not concerned about whether this action is big enough to change your level of health. (We can build on that later; for now, we just need to start.) We specifically are assessing the action based on your context.

Here are suggestions of actions associated with the example pillars:

- Boundaries: Say "no" or "I'll think about it," not "yes"
- Self-care: Do a two-minute meditation once per week; schedule a walk with a friend once, then schedule the next one
- Commitment: Insert protected time for a goal in your daily schedule
- Simplicity: Do a 20 percent version of most things first
- Daring more often: If unsure, try
- Relationships: Schedule one connection per week

We don't want
an unrealistic
plan you do not
implement;
we want a
realistic plan you
start today.

———————

- Mindfulness: Schedule and protect five minutes each morning for mindfulness practice or reading

- Recovery: Put vacations in the calendar for the next twelve months; when accepting an engagement, add prep time in the calendar right away; track how long it takes you to do things

If You Did This in Your Head

Les paroles s'envolent, les écrits restent. (Spoken words fly away, written words remain.)

Quite possibly, you may have already pictured this exercise in your head. It may be relatively clear to you now, but what if you tried to recall it in two weeks? You would likely have to do the work again. The same way most exercises and homework in cognitive behavior therapy are written, this one is more likely to propel you forward if you take fifteen minutes (set an alarm on your phone) to put your ideas down on paper. Particularly when you put ideas together in a new way, writing them on paper may give you a different perspective, a distance that can lead to a clearer analysis and more effective actions. And you won't have to re-create it in two weeks.

You now have your plan. The reality is that your life is already very full. You can only realistically implement a small number of actions that are customized to your own context. What is extremely important is that you start with one action.

Communicate Your Plan

Heard from a senior professional as she approached implementing her plan: "If I sit on the couch doing nothing for even five minutes, my family will be shocked."

Sabrina had started to put her plan together, confident that she needed to infuse "air" in her 24/7 work and nonwork life. She was also apprehensive about whether she would physically be able to do it, how her family would react, and, deep down, if her family would still value her. She realized that one thing she needed to do was communicate with those around her, possibly even at work, about her plan.

Whether at work or in your personal life, you operate within a system, and if you've created a new plan for yourself, it will likely lead to changes in your choices and actions, which may be noticed by and influence others. Depending on your relationship with them, it may be useful and even more effective to talk about it. The act of sharing it may also serve as a commitment in itself and generate additional support.

Malika had been on medical leave and was just returning on the day that I was doing a virtual keynote for her group of seventy leaders. Her senior leader was there, as were most of her peers. This was one of the rare times when this group would carve out time to be together. Before getting started, I noticed how close this group was. People said hello to each other in the chat and commented with humor on their backgrounds and cats. Then, their senior leader started with welcoming comments, shared his own challenges with the demands of going through a pandemic, welcomed new team members, and invited them to say a few words.

When he asked if he had missed anyone, Malika raised her hand. She turned on her camera and smiled. "I am so glad to be back, everyone. This is my first day back, and it could not be a better way for me to return. One thing I want to tell you all is that I am thrilled to be here and that I have learned an important lesson through this chapter. From now on, I will always protect my health first. I love my work and I love my health even more. That's it! Looking forward to reconnecting with you all and to today's talk."

Consider the various stakeholders involved in the contexts in which you are looking to make changes. The impacts of your changes and the communication may vary with people you have a different type and depth of relationship with. You might start with those with whom you have a closer relationship. The content of the communication can be fairly simple. For example, "I have committed to a goal of building and protecting my health even more, so I have made the commitment to respect clear boundaries between my work hours and non-work hours. I know that in the past I have responded to emails anytime I could. My new approach will be to focus on my work during work hours, including responses to emails. If something is time-sensitive outside of work hours, let's call each other."

Sometimes people worry about the size of the impact of their change or worry that the change will be so historically uncharacteristic of them that it might hurt their "personal brand." As you look at your values, you will likely find that your previous approach only partially reflected your values and that the new approach you designed aligns better. Many have been surprised by the refreshing ease with which a well-aligned plan can allow values to be lived even more fully. This approach will be most useful also in communications with your employer, whether with your manager or HR partner, and with the people close to you in your personal life.

Professional Context

The exact nature of what, when, and with whom you communicate at work will vary based on several things. Some of these variables may include how much you trust the person and to what degree your new plan will involve significant changes in your approach to your work. Sometimes, the decision to communicate is part of your own accountability plan: If you tell your peers at a team meeting that, moving forward, you will manage meetings you lead to end five minutes early, you might find yourself sticking to your plan even more. Whatever your plan is, it may be good to get feedback from a few people you trust, potentially including using professional resources you can access (such as an executive coach, mentor, or counselor) to identify any blind spots, assumptions, and expectations you did not realize you had.

California-based board chair, executive coach, and HR consultant Cindy Kaczmarek has worked with countless leaders and shared with me how both professionals and leaders immensely benefit from being intentional and acting as needed regarding their resilience. She wants people to ask, "Who does your counseling?" the same way they discuss other services. (Very Californian of her, even if she is originally from Canada!) The more these conversations are easily incorporated into your work culture, the better. This is a contribution that most of us can make now—it can be as simple as transparently mentioning you had an appointment last week with your preferred professional resource: "Thanks for your flexibility on our meeting, I had a pre-scheduled appointment with my [counselor/psychologist/coach/mentor] at that time."

In Your Personal Life

It might be good to share your plan with people you have a close relationship with. The decision to communicate and how much to say will likely be connected with where you are at in your relationship and the degree to which your changes might affect it. Assuming that you have a good level of trust in the person and that some of your changes involve changes in your relationship, here are a few suggestions for this conversation:

- Proactively mention that you would like to have a chat to share some of your personal resilience plans; decide together when might be a good time.

You may tell yourself
that you can't
possibly need help
to design something
that should be so
obvious. The reality
is that it's not.

———————————

- Give them background for how you got there, potentially sharing the link with your values.

- Share some of your planned actions and what you would like to ask from them, if anything (for example, "I need you to not comment on whether I am doing this or not"; "I would love for you to mention it if you see me do it"; "I will commit to updating you from time to time on how I'm implementing my actions, but on my own time").

- Check in with them in terms of what they may need from you, how they are doing, et cetera. Keep in mind that they may not have similar intentions and don't need to have them.

Getting a Consultant

You may tell yourself that you can't possibly need help to design something that should be so obvious. The reality is that it's not. It is a science and an art. In your own work you likely at times hire and work with consultants when you need particular expertise. Your resilience functions the same way. If you feel you could use support along the way or to clear the initial fog, or even if you're wondering if you should, connecting with a resource earlier rather than later is often best. You may find support both informally via people close to you whom you trust and formally via regulated professionals, such as registered psychologists (types of formal registration vary across and sometimes within countries) and others.

Sabrina, who had predicted that her family would be shocked if she sat on the couch doing nothing for five minutes, came back at her next session beaming. "I had a particularly challenging day at work on Tuesday and decided that instead of rushing to my evening duties, I would sit in front of the fire for thirty minutes, just looking at it. And I did. Both my kids and my husband came to me asking if I was okay, and I told them I was, that I just needed to sit and do nothing for a bit. Nothing terrible happened. I felt both deliciously delinquent and refreshed. I will do this again for sure."

Your Next Action (15 minutes)

As you approach creating this first version of your Custom Strategic Resilience Plan, you may want it to be inclusive and perfect, but then what happens? You hold off on finishing it. You need to do the opposite: Don't expect perfection. Simplify and write something now. What would you tell someone in a similar situation? You'd probably tell them to make a first draft. Same here. Keep in mind what I often say to my clients: "Anything is better than nothing." Just put some ideas down on paper.

To complete this exercise, I suggest you protect a minimum of fifteen minutes of your time. Set an alarm on your phone right now. You might be surprised how much you complete. If you wish, you can set aside a bit more time later; this will probably be at the most one hour. Allowing more time later gives you space and may allow incubation to take place, which can help when you're creating.

Have your completed Supply/Demands Inventory (Activity Sheet 1) in front of you, because this will inform you where to go next. Use your Priority Values List (Activity Sheet 2) to guide your reflection. My main recommendation is that you do this in writing, as opposed to just in your head, because it will be easier to stay focused and you won't have to re-create it later.

Go to the Custom Strategic Resilience Plan in Appendix B (Activity Sheet 4):

1 Identify three key pillars, or categories of action (see the examples on page 108). You need clarity on what these are to support the movement toward your goals.

2 For each pillar, identify a few actions that would bring this particular pillar to life. This is necessary to guide your next steps.

3 Think of one person you might want to communicate your plan with. This will be critical both for them to understand the changes they see and in order for them to support you.

4 Circle the one action under one of the pillars that you're going to start implementing between now and next week, ideally today. Once implemented, maintain this one and add another from your plan.

Questions for Reflection

• What is one of your pillars?

• For which pillar do you need additional ideas to translate into actions?

• If you were to connect with an additional resource tomorrow, where would you look first?

Remember

- A plan is more than a few ideas of generic actions semi-implemented.

- Your plan is specific to you and your context.

- Use your own information from previous chapters, including the Supply/Demands Inventory, Priority Values List, and Quadrants of Context, to choose your three to five strategic pillars.

- Your strategic pillars will translate into realistic actions. Strategy is only as strong as its execution.

- Smaller actions are more doable. Try for a realistic plan that you can start on today.

- "Done" is better than "perfect." Write a draft of your plan now. Writing your plan makes it more real.

- Communicate about your plan with key people.

- You've done some hard work during this chapter designing your Custom Strategic Resilience Plan. Take a moment and congratulate yourself!

—[7]—

Implement Your Strategic Resilience Plan

One of the debates in business strategy is about determining which is most important: strategy or execution. Is it best to have a solid strategy, and execution can be average, or to have an average strategy executed strongly? We could easily fall into thinking that if we have a strategy, execution will (or should) naturally occur. Not the case. You will need to not only evolve your strategy over time, because things change, but also actively manage the execution of your strategy. I have seen first-hand over my years as a psychologist, consultant, and executive coach that successful execution connects strongly with a strategy.

Vic is a highly specialized, in-demand professional. They had designed their plan carefully and successfully implemented it over twenty-four months. Then, Vic came to me saying they had "no momentum." One of their pillars was physical health, and one action was doing four thirty-minute cardio workouts per week. Most weeks they had successfully implemented this and felt great about it. Yet now they had "no momentum."

I asked a bit more about the context. Since when, and what had changed in that timeframe? Turns out that in the previous five weeks, the work demands from their various contracts had all increased at the same time temporarily, so they had worked twelve-hour days every day. Initially they were able to maintain the physical activity cadence, but they rapidly found themselves at best making it two times per week, and sometimes once only.

I asked them what they would say to a colleague if their colleague told them, "I used to exercise four times per week, but in the past five weeks I've worked twelve-hour days and only exercised once or twice per week."

"I'd say that's amazing," they said.

They had maintained momentum, but had just adapted it to a new context in which the demands were significantly different from those considered when the plan was designed. For Vic, we discussed the benefits of having a second version of their plan because, while these phases were rare, they had happened before and were likely to happen again. The second version took minutes to create because Vic now had clarity. Having the plan, however, put Vic back in a more mindful and deliberate place because of the realistic appraisal of their new context, in addition to continuing to build their self-efficacy.

By nature, your current plan is specific to your current context. Your goal and your values may remain relatively stable, but the sources of supply and demands and the internal and external forces affecting your context may change.

Remember, you are creating a plan that is unique to you, just as your DNA molecule is unique to you. As you grow, and as you encounter new challenges, your "helix" will twist and turn to stay stable and strong as you adapt it to new contexts.

Optimize the Implementation of Your Plan

You have your goal, your strategic pillars, and your actions. Strategy is only as strong as its execution. While all the conscious efforts we make in crafting realistic and achievable goals are necessary, we now know from research that we can have an impact on the less conscious parts of our brain to move us toward our goals.

There is a lot that your brain decides for you without your conscious input. This is very adaptive, given the millions of decision points we encounter every day. One interesting and important fact is that these decisions happening without our input are not always on message, aligned with what we've set out to do consciously. If you've ever taken a test to discover your unconscious biases, you likely discovered that despite the fact that you hold very clear values consciously, your test results revealed choices that are not aligned with these values. For our purposes, this means that the more we can support the subconscious processes in the direction of our goal, the better.

Choice architecture has been studied by Dr. Wendy Wood, an expert on habits. The concept refers to creating a context that helps you make choices aligned with your goal. Concretely, this means setting things up in your environment so it will be even easier for your brain to take the actions you set out to accomplish.

Ben had made a commitment to himself to bring yoga into his morning routine. He knew and had experienced the benefits. Yet the habit was not taking root. He then decided to implement as many aspects of a choice architecture around this action as he could. Going through his morning routine, he placed his yoga clothes between his bed and his bedroom door, laid his yoga mat out at its specific location the night before, and had his yoga app ready to launch. As research has predicted, he found himself turning his intention into action, at times for a very short time, but with a frequency that was much higher.

Jess had made a personal commitment to manage actively the work demands coming their way. This involved receiving requests and systematically responding either with a decline or with an engagement to look at this new demand in the context of other demands and to get back to the requester with an update in twenty-four hours. To support this choice, Jess had template email responses and had developed a verbal response that they practiced and had written on a note by their computer, so it would be easily accessible. When going to work in person, they used an elastic band on their wrist to serve as a physical reminder and symbol that the ratio of demands and supply could be over-stretched and required their active management. The habit of accepting

all new demands had been strong for Jess, but this reminder
and the additional step in their response process was what
they needed to slow them down just enough to align their
behavior with their values and plan.

Recent literature, particularly the work of Dr. Gary
Latham, has paired the well-established goal-setting theory
with the concept of priming. Priming refers to exposing your
brain to a word or image (research suggests that an image
is likely to be more powerful). The goal-setting theory is
something you likely use already, formally or informally: you
may, for example, set clear goals that are high enough to be
motivating but not so high they're impossible. You are also
probably aware of the SMART acronym: specific, measurable,
achievable, realistic, timely. All this is conscious. The concept
of priming is a process that operates without our conscious
effort. New research has paired these with fascinating results.

In what is now a famous study, researchers posted a photo
of a woman winning a race—so a high-performance priming—
in a call center where workers were doing fundraising. Control groups saw either no photo or other photos, and the
researchers didn't tell the participants what they were doing,
so they did not know they were primed. The individuals who
had the high-performance priming photo in front of them as
they made the calls raised 60 percent more money than the
others. Imagine that bar chart! Very statistically and materially significant. And this is just one study to demonstrate the
point. This has been replicated in laboratories, organizations,
and teams, and the effects have been consistently observed.

My client Lisa had planned to incorporate meditation into her life for a few years. Then, she decided to pair conscious goal-setting with priming, so she clarified for herself the moment, duration, and application she would use, and she posted a picture of someone meditating close to her workspace. As predicted, she was finally able to incorporate a meditation practice into her life. She still had weeks with lower frequency, but the practice became a standing part of her schedule and still is to this day.

The point is that priming is likely to have a positive effect and can be used personally and in organizations. Of course, we already know from research that the goals need to be set in a certain way. They do need to be achievable, for example. Provided your goals are set appropriately, and still managed consciously, priming can help. You can see it as adding wind at your back.

Planning for Sustainability

You have worked to create your strategy, and you know it will need to evolve over time. Planning now for the sustainability of your strategy will help prepare you. One key is to carry with you into the future what you have learned now. This is because you might start feeling very confident about your resilience and gradually let go of actions that contributed to it being so strong. You might let go of checking in with yourself frequently and proactively, so you may miss early signs that your resilience is trending down. And you might not see quickly that you need to act, or which actions to take, until your resilience is much lower than where you wanted. But you can get ahead of all this. Let's crystalize what you've just done so you can capture what has worked for you and keep it with you into the future. Answer these three questions (ideally in writing):

1 What have you done so far as a result of this book that has helped? List all the concrete actions you have taken.

2 How will you know if your resilience is trending down?

3 What will you do if you notice this? List as many concrete actions as you can think of.

Your responses to these questions become your own guide. How solidly you plan for and incorporate flexibility will, in part, predict how successfully you manage sustainability.

Sustainability will also require agility, which may include having a Plan B. While your overall context will at times remain relatively stable, small aspects of it will likely vary on a day-to-day basis. It is not possible to forecast everything. This is why having a Plan B for your actions is critical. By having a Plan B, I am referring to creating—at times on the spot—a modified version of your plan that you are able to implement in some form today. Because anything is better than nothing.

Beth, whom I introduced in Chapter 1, found this tip particularly useful. She had found herself semi-implementing her actions, and given massive demands from her work life, she realized that she had been trying for over a year to hire a team member she desperately needed. She wanted to do this well, and in the absence of having enough time had been delaying this important action. Her Plan B was to work at it consistently but gradually, investing ten minutes per week first thing every Monday to identify a small, two-minute action she would take each day that week. When she switched to identifying one action so small that she could take it each day, she found herself gaining traction.

One month later, she was beaming. "I made myself do a two-minute task on this every day before my lunch (using an alarm on my phone) and identifying what my action would be for the following day. I am happy to report that I have interviews lined up!" During the first week, she used her Monday time to list what information she already had and what was missing. Her task for Tuesday was to locate one piece of information that she thought she had (her wish list of qualifications). On Wednesday, it was to locate a posting she had used before, and Thursday's was to come up with a list of people in her network to whom she would send the posting first in case they knew someone. On Friday, she drafted the email she would send them.

The nudge to switch to a Plan B worked for her, and feedback that many others have shared with me has shown the same.

We want to stay adaptive, agile. A plan that is rigid is not going to be a good plan. We know this from research on habits: You want to ideally keep everything the same—same action, same time, same place—to facilitate a habit. However, research has also identified that it is critical to have flexibility, because if anything deviates from the specific plan and it's not flexible, then the habit stops. What we want is a version of the habit to remain, hence having flexibility in your plan. If your action is to go for at least a fifteen-minute walk once a day, for example, and on a certain day you just cannot, then have a Plan B. Don't just drop it. The Plan B may be to stand outside and take five deep breaths, then come back in. Or it could be to stand by your desk and step in place for a minute. Think of this alternate implementation not so much for its value as exercise, but instead for maintaining the habit. Which, in the end, will help with its value as exercise.

What Gets Measured Gets Done—and Celebrated

One distinct action often separates individuals for whom habit forming works and for whom it does not: monitoring. We know from research that just monitoring an action is likely to improve its implementation. This is true in business, but it's also true in your personal life. Put this to your advantage with an easy-to-implement measurement approach. It may be as simple as taking a moment at the end of every day to note with a checkmark that you took your key action, per your plan. Or noting in your agenda the specific action you took that day; for example, how long you meditated.

If you really want to take this to the next level, you may want to consider a structured planner or journal like the

Daily Resilience Planner I mentioned in Chapter 3, in which you note for a maximum of one minute your actions for the day (see Appendix A). Specifically, at the beginning of the day you note which actions you'll take that day, given your schedule. At the end of the day, you note what you did, in addition to a win and something you learned (if any). At the end of each week, you flip through your notes and extract one win and one lesson. At the end of each month, you look at your four weekly summaries and extract the top wins and learnings to take with you as you continue to move forward. The advantage of this approach is that, particularly for competitive individuals constantly looking at what they need to achieve next, and with a tendency to recognize others' accomplishments but not their own, it ensures they take in their wins and learnings and keeps them following their strategic resilience plan.

I often see this opportunity in my executive coaching work. Very driven professionals and leaders often move to the next goal as soon as they've reached one, no matter how significant. In doing so, they not only miss the opportunity to celebrate, but also miss the opportunity for their brain to learn and anchor the new path, an important step in making it easier to travel forward.

When Jack came back to me after having built his strategic resilience plan and expressed how, for the first time in his entire life, he had approached a challenge entirely differently simply by adding a fifteen-minute buffer to it, he was very pleased with his success. I then asked him to "stay there" a bit longer and describe the feeling he had.

Strategy is only as strong as its execution.

"Better than stress!" he said. "I actually felt really happy. Proud. Profoundly respectful of the other person and of myself."

Now, that's some motivation to try this again.

Circumstances Change: Adjust Your Plan

I am originally from Québec City on the east coast of Canada, where winters come with temperatures of minus 22 Fahrenheit (minus 30 Celsius) or colder. Visitors (and many locals) often complain how cold this is. For those who don't complain, the approach is often along the lines of, "You just need to dress for it." When circumstances change, values and goals remain, but supply and demands are often different, so your plan needs to be modified. If you keep the same plan (or the same coat), it might not work so well.

Circumstances will change, sometimes predictably, but often unexpectedly. Given that our brain has a preference for and a bias toward keeping the status quo, even when we could have predicted that our circumstances are likely to change, we don't think about it. It's a matter of, "Too busy; we'll cross that river when we get to it." Examples may include a finance professional knowing that the end of the fiscal year is systematically a very busy and demanding time; a teacher knowing that by February the energy of September is a faint flame; a management consultant who sees how key projects will all culminate in a busy phase at the same time. You know when these times may come, and so far, you've accepted these times as "the dark period" to just get through and try to survive.

For many, the way they'll realize that circumstances have changed is they'll realize their actions are not getting implemented the way they used to, or at all. Some will then ignore the plan and avoid thinking about it; others may blame themselves for the lack of successful implementation and feel not only less resilient but also incompetent, a failure. None of this helps.

The reality is that a change in circumstances often comes with a change in demands and, potentially, supply, whether it is naturally part of the new context or it represents an opportunity for you to implement a change. Having visibility as early as possible in this process can be the difference between surviving and thriving, or at least between burning out and making it out okay.

Even if circumstances change, your values are likely relatively stable. Your goal can also remain relatively stable, or evolve over time. What is critical is to realize, preferably proactively, that the context will or has changed, ideally realizing this as early as possible. One way to get ahead is to schedule a regular check-in with yourself to reassess often. A frequent barrier to this habit is the amount of time your brain tells you it's going to take (and that you don't have); however, you need to ensure you are realistic and treat this as an experiment. The reassessment can be as short as two minutes on a weekly or monthly basis, with the frequency depending on how many changes you are going through.

In case of doubt, however, reassess often, such as once per week.

Once you realize that circumstances have changed, most people's brains will still want to stay with the status quo and try to stick to the unmodified plan. This may be a form of persistence that has been possible in the past; earlier in your career, perhaps, when the combination of demands allowed for that elasticity. If at this point the implementation is suffering, the more realistic and ultimately self-efficacious next step is to modify the plan. There is truly no point trying to "stick to the plan no matter what." This approach would be analogous to having a gym-based exercise program that you've done before and that you're trying to stick to even if you're coming back to training after an injury. You may just hurt yourself. You need a new version.

Circumstance and context changes can come in many forms. One is when a family member is living with a health issue. Marty's partner, Lindsay, was recently diagnosed with post-traumatic stress disorder (PTSD). While Lindsay was receiving therapy for her PTSD, her mom was unexpectedly diagnosed with terminal cancer. This situation understandably exacerbated Lindsay's PTSD symptoms, with impacts on many aspects of her life.

As her partner, Marty had participated in an early therapy session to learn how best to support Lindsay. Given that things had changed, Marty asked if she could join again to best adjust. She also knew that these new demands on

Lindsay would likely require more support from her, which she very much wanted to provide, and that she would have her own reactions to Lindsay's emotions and also her own grief associated with Lindsay's mother. She modified her plan proactively to keep versions of her actions and added new ones specific to her circumstances.

Vacation is probably one of the most insidious types of context change. It is one that is typically planned, positive, and expected to go well. That expectation in itself may sometimes need to be realistically assessed. If everyone is joining the vacation already drained, they will unlikely be at their best; activities, even those we choose and love, require energy; if we have not had explicit conversations about hopes for the vacation, different people are more likely than not to have slightly different needs and wants. These problems are true not only for extended vacations, but also for weekend getaways.

Scott and Kristy had planned a weekend getaway. They both had worked many more hours than usual and had done so in their cozy but small condo. They had decided to stay at a resort, expecting to be in a calm, spa-like environment where they could have both a bit of individual time and time together. The resort turned out to be very busy with guests, many of whom were on the louder side. This irritated them, leading to less-than-pleasant verbal exchanges with each other. They then realized that to make the most of this time away, they had to change their plans. They researched other activities around the resort, created a new schedule for themselves that involved spending most of the time outside, and ended up coming back refreshed and happy with their adventure.

Emergencies (including public health emergencies such as a pandemic), disasters (natural and others), and violent events represent significant demands in terms of coping. On the one hand, these are obvious changes in circumstances that could affect us; on the other hand, the fact that they may be experienced by many others can lead us to disregard them as a circumstance we need to adjust to and actively cope with. In other words, we might tell ourselves it's fine because others are going through it, even when it is having an impact.

Ming was at the beginning of a three-year contract when a pandemic started. They were at a good place from both personal and professional perspectives. Being in health care, Ming knew that, for them to be able to continue to support their patients, they had to frontload and maintain a bona fide attention to their resilience. While Ming's original plan involved weekly physical activity, the occasional drink, and relatively healthy nutrition, they knew they had to change this, at least in the short term. They created a schedule for themselves that they would review on a weekly basis.

Circumstances are bound to change, and our brain is bound to favor the status quo. Therefore, a frequent assessment of whether circumstances have changed or might change, paired with modifications to your plan, is likely to keep you on track to work toward your goals, in addition to maintaining and growing your sense of self-efficacy.

Versions of Your Plan

You may need a few different versions of your plan that factor in various circumstances: the plan you already have, another one for when the kids are home, and one for when you're on vacation, for example. Lana had separated from her partner in the past year, and they had a shared parenting agreement for their fourteen-year-old boy, alternating each week. In her line of work, taking large chunks of vacation was easier and allowed her to match her son's school schedule.

As I supported Lana through a mental health disability work absence, she designed her first plan. Rapidly, she realized that she would need a second plan for the weeks when her son was with her. That week offered different sources of demands (such as driving her son to and from extracurricular activities) and sources of supply (such as conversations with her son and activities they liked to share, and opportunities for her to be physically active while her son was at his activities). Later, she realized she also needed a one-time version for extended vacation, which she easily created.

Connecting With a Resource

If you've tried designing and implementing your plan and, despite your strong desire to see a change, you are just not implementing it for some reason, this may be the time to connect with a resource. If the focus is related to work performance, working with an executive coach will give you "another head working with you on the situation" and the support you need. If the focus is related to psychological health, working with a regulated professional such as a psychologist will help you gain perspective and identify how to change the ways you think, feel, and act to better align with your goals. A good place to start is to connect with a physical health regulated professional, like a physician or nurse practitioner, who will often be aware of resources in your community or how to find them.

Your Next Action (5 minutes)

Identify one aspect discussed in this chapter that might be relevant to your plan. This may be the need to have a Plan B for when things get busy or the need for another version of your plan. Note how you will manage change when it happens.

Question for Reflection

- What is one circumstance in your life that will soon call for a different version of your plan?

Remember

- Treat your strategy and actions as a plan in constant evolution.

- Take actions to nourish the plan and celebrate successes.

- Even positive events (such as vacation or children's school breaks) can mean you need to adjust your plan.

- Put review times in your calendar so you can identify when you're on track and when you need to modify your plan.

— [8]—

When You Need a Leave of Absence

How many times have you said to yourself or your co-workers, "I just need a break"? Are you at a point now where you need one? Needing a break is not the same as needing a leave of absence, but it raises a flag. Ignoring this flag may get you to the point where the only option is a leave of absence.

Our mental health is on a continuum, and within this continuum is the mental illness range. There is a part of this range where our level of functioning may be affected to the point that we cannot work. This is when we may need to go on a medical leave, in this case for mental health reasons. In the workplace, mental health–related absences are mostly related to what we call "common disorders." These disorders typically include mood, anxiety, adjustment, and substance-use disorders.

You may not have been on such a medical leave, or you may have. But even if you have not, you know it exists, like a black box that doesn't belong to you. True, this is the area of expertise of registered psychologists and other health professionals. But knowing how to protect your mental health anywhere on the continuum changes everything, for every-one. The more information and literacy you have, the more you'll have visibility on your situation at any given point in time and can take actions proactively.

One of the mechanisms by which literacy operates is by helping increase our self-efficacy, a concept developed by Dr. Albert Bandura. Self-efficacy is something we know from goal-setting theory that affects our ability to take action. But we lack personal knowledge about what happens during a leave of absence, so we make assumptions that can become obstacles. As I talked about in Chapter 3, these are unhelpful thinking patterns we must change to ensure evidence-based thinking. And to ensure we have confidence in knowing that we are doing the most effective and ethical thing, and that our actions and choices today support positive results.

Let's visit the disability range of the mental health contin-uum. There are two myths related to mental health disability absences that are critical to address. The first myth is that a leave of absence is like a holiday. Most people believe this. I have heard partners of clients initially say to my clients who have just started a leave, "You'll have a lot on your to-do list while you are off!"

This is a typical reaction, since this is the only reference point most people have. Some clients even think this for themselves—they are finally away from work, so they can just be like they are when taking a few days off! However, they quickly come to realize that they can't do much of anything because their energy is too low or they are dealing with a combination of symptoms that makes this time anything but a vacation. What I help my clients—and will hopefully help you—realize is that it's the same as if you are dealing with a physical health issue. This is time off work to take care of your health.

Heard from the physician of a client who suffered a knee injury while skiing during a mental health disability absence: "Look at you, skiing and all. That's nice!" The client started crying, as it had taken everything she had to make herself go, and now she had a physical injury to deal with in addition to her depression. What many people don't know is that doing pleasurable activities is part of treatment.

The reality is that during this time off work, the individual is paid to follow treatment plans designed by their health team, which typically includes a physician or nurse practitioner and a psychologist.

The second myth is that being off work will be all that's needed to recover and rebuild health. In early phases of experiencing mental health challenges, taking a long weekend or a vacation can often be enough to replenish and build back your energy. However, when we are so unwell that we take a leave for health reasons, simply being off work is not sufficient.

If the person off work is left without active treatment, they are not only at risk of not recovering optimally (or at all), but they are also missing an opportunity to build their self-efficacy. I have observed in my work, as have many others, including the Canadian Society of Professionals in Disability Management, that the longer someone is off, the more they're at risk of not returning. This is where having prior literacy helps, because it means that even as the person's mental health is declining, they get a sense of the importance of connecting with resources before leaving work.

Preventing and Supporting Absences Due to Mental Health Disability

Given enough demands, anyone can burn out. Having mental health disability prevention and management literacy can help you personally and help you support others. Whether you work for an employer who provides short- and long-term disability coverage or are self-employed with other types of "safety nets," the preferred state is to stay at work, assuming that you are healthy enough to be there.

Sometimes, individuals and health professionals, including physicians and psychologists, assume that a person must leave an environment that may have fully, or even in part, contributed to the demands that created the imbalance. This kind of decision is at times the recommended approach, but it is often not the best approach and needs to be assessed carefully. In our conversation, Tennessee-based clinical and consulting psychologist Dr. Les Kertay, who is also senior vice president of behavioral health at Axiom Medical, shared that "many health professionals recommend avoidance of work when an individual is experiencing work-related challenges." And I agree; I have seen the same. The reality is that an absence from work may at times be needed, but many other times what is needed is to find a solution to the situation. A lot of this power is in the hands of the individual, even if the cause of the problem may be within the work.

What's important for you to know is that when you reach a point at which your health is insufficient to be at work, it usually means that you are in a fairly intense level of pain that affects your level of functioning. Ideally, you'll proactively work to not reach this point, although if you do, remember that there will be supports to help you recover. If your health allows you to stay at work, this is the recommended action.

The idea of being off work, away from all those demands, may feel attractive initially. The reality of finding yourself on disability often is not. I regularly need to support my clients through the fact that they are on a health leave in itself, in addition to supporting them returning to health. Keep in mind that remaining off work on disability is hardly the goal for most people. Therefore, in this section, we'll look at mental health disability prevention, what happens while you or someone you know is on disability, the return-to-work process, and four key trends on the horizon for mental health disability management.

Before: Prevention through the Power of Mental Health Literacy

In the early part of the mental health continuum, prevention is possible. The support people have in their workplace and in their personal life is a significant variable in the overall mental health equation. Support often reduces the need for an absence and can promote a fast recovery. But to provide that support, we need to have mental health literacy. The employer has a role to play here; you as an individual also have this opportunity.

Low resource utilization was shown to be connected— both in work by Dr. Jennifer Dimoff and Dr. Kevin Kelloway and in practice—to three main reasons that point to why employees fail to use available resources:

1   Lack of recognition that they could benefit from them

2   Lack of awareness that they can use these resources for themselves

3   Fear of being stigmatized or discriminated against for using the resources

These three reasons can be reduced to two main barriers: poor levels of knowledge about resources and stigma. Stigma can be reduced by educating employees on mental illnesses, warning signs associated with poor mental health, and available resources and sources of support. Both managers and coworkers can aid in the "resource use" process by providing direct support and improving awareness of those resources. Specific training may, for example, focus on the most prevalent mental health issues, such as depression, anxiety, and substance use.

Workplace mental health involves the organization, teams, and individuals. When looking at supporting the mental health of our colleagues, our team members, and ourselves, we want to think of our workplace in an integrative way. The component that will make this integration more effective is deep clarity on the interrelations between the organization's human resources policies and practices and the individual employees. Individual employees should feel they are partners and co-creators of the organization's human resources system. There is an interplay between the various factors of workforce mental health because this reciprocal interaction is now widely accepted based on research.

During: Improve Support

Despite the best support efforts of colleagues, teams, and organizations, some employees will need a mental health disability absence. That can raise questions. What happens during these leaves? What factors are linked to a better recovery? What opportunities do you have to improve outcomes—your own and those of others?

How does it feel to go on leave? Vicky is a health care worker who was taken off work by her physician for four weeks for mental health reasons. Here is what she told me: "I am here, on day one, alone at home sitting at the kitchen table. I'm feeling at my lowest, and I now have the additional challenge of being off work, which brings a mix of relief because I could not do anything else than this, but also guilt in leaving the team, and fear of what's next for me. I'm feeling very alone in this, with little control and a fear that I may never get better." It did get better for Vicky a few weeks later, and she successfully returned to work after one extension of her leave, but this is how it initially felt.

When someone is off work, everyone around them can be part of the solution, whether their manager, their coworker, their case manager, or in any other role. You don't want to sit back and wait for them to return to work. Each touch point is an opportunity to be an even better part of the solution. If you have to be in touch because of your role, you may, for example, say something like, "Just want you to know that we look forward to having you back, whenever that is." Or you may send a note or card with a supportive and positive message of what you appreciate about them. If you send an email to their personal email address, it's okay to add that you don't expect them to respond; that you just wanted them to know you're thinking about them.

Julie Menten is an employment lawyer who often sees conflictual situations occur as a result of misconceptions in high-performance cultures; these misconceptions do not support being proactive. Things can get more problematic and become adversarial, when a proactive approach might have led to a different and likely healthier process and solution. Getting there, she says, becomes possible in cultures that invest in a mental health strategy. From an individual perspective, having your own strategy will help you manage your part in this relationship, regardless of whether the work culture you are in has decided to manage its part.

The first myth is
that a leave
of absence is like
a holiday.

———————

After: Maintain Support

Imagine that you're returning to work after a mental health–related absence. How do you know if you're ready to return—and that your employer is ready too? Research has uncovered several factors and best practices that can positively affect the outcome. There are key themes associated with a successful return to work, and everyone can contribute an action to support themselves and others in this important transition.

If someone has been off work for health reasons, they may benefit from a certain context for successful return. Why do we need a certain "context"? The main reason is that, when we're dealing with mental health issues, treatment will only get us so far. The last part of recovery requires exposure to work demands. If that exposure is both manageable and supportive, we are more likely to build a successful adaptation.

It's important to remember that for most mental health–related absences, individuals are not at 100 percent when they begin the return-to-work phase. When someone is off work, the focus becomes returning to health, and this is true whether the causes are personal health difficulties or organizational problems. There will be times when characteristics of the workplace caused, whether mostly or partially, the health issues. When this is the case, the causal factors need to receive attention. Sometimes, even if workplace characteristics were not causal as far as we can tell, the contextual variables may benefit from attention—we can see this as continuous improvement.

Let's assume that the individual is now ready to proceed with a return to work. What are some actions that can lead to success? Here are a few actions to consider:

- That the return to work be gradual.

- That accommodations be considered as needed. This is in recognition of the fact that a gradual return likely involves a modified workload. But it also recognizes that the work setting may be a contributing factor to the mental health issue.

- That everyone involved, including the person off work, protects the return-to-work plan, and that "work creep" and added pressures don't begin.

- That the individual believes they can successfully return to work (self-efficacy).

Whether you are a coworker or a supervisor, you can have a positive impact here. The more proactive you can be—for example, via mental health disability literacy—the better.

Optimism and Your Future Self

Insurance carriers create models that allow them to predict, with relative precision for large groups of individuals, the proportion who will deal with any given issue they are insuring for. They manage risk. Take life, for example. Longevity can be predicted using key variables, such as current age, gender, and health status. Once the prediction has been made, the insurance carrier creates the financial reserves that will allow them to provide the coverage they are hired to provide.

Our human brain has a strong tendency to think in the short term. Yet, a broader perspective would bring information that we need now. If we are currently in November, deciding to renovate the kitchen in March seems manageable. When adding details from a more informed, forward-looking perspective—you're pregnant and giving birth in June; you work in accounting, with the fiscal year ending in March; and renovations typically go longer than planned—bringing significantly more demands your way at the same time, you might pause.

In managing your mental health, an informed, forward-looking approach helps ensure that you give yourself as much visibility as possible on the supply and demands you are likely to experience. There will still be uncertainty. The trap that most fall into is believing that because there is uncertainty, there is no point forecasting or planning. That it's best to just go day by day with your instincts and past learnings from experience.

Our mental health will be affected by several variables, many of which are outside of our direct control, like genetics or an imbalance in the brain. There are also variables we do have control over. The missing link for many is the motivation to act, to protect and nourish our mental health. It's as if in the moment we disregard any other variable in the equation and add more to our plate. A moment later we realize this was not a good idea as the rest of the variables in the equation become visible again, but we put our head down and push forward.

To forecast accurately, you need to look at all the data. Once an insurance carrier has identified the set of variables that best predict a potential outcome, they would not use just one of the variables. They would use all of them. The human brain is at risk of using only part of the model, but whenever you find yourself using all of it, you'll be ahead.

You own the responsibility to ensure your mental wellness, to "insure" and create reserves. Only you have the most accurate equation for modeling your situation. You know your sources of demands and sources of supply. Forecasting is still not going to be exact because no one has complete information, but using the information you, and only you, have is power in your hands to increase your own self-efficacy and optimism, two concepts that support resilience.

One challenge I often ask my clients to consider is the following. You have created a realistic list of your sources of supply and demands, both professional and personal. When an additional demand of significance appears (even the most exciting ones), do not say "yes" immediately. If you believe it is a "no," perfect; you can say "no" now. That's usually not the issue. If you feel you have to say "yes," then instead say something like, "I want to say yes, but let me look at my current list and get back to you tomorrow." Then, respond the next day after considering your list of supply and demands. This protects you against the very human tendency to focus on the present. We tend to go for the short-term reward ("They'll think I am great") rather than choosing the long-term benefits ("I love this project and wish I could help but would first need to see what else needs to be deprioritized").

Whenever clients try this, they often report two key discoveries. First, they feel fabulous, in control, and grounded— any version of self-efficacy, a derivative of believing that you can have an impact on your situation in the here and now. In the academic literature and as a human experience, self-efficacy is gold. Second, they are surprised by how easy this was. They communicated their bottom line and how they were going to manage the demand, and they did it. As simple as that. They can do it again. Self-efficacy is, in theory and practice, in part how optimism emerges: through the belief that you'll be able to have an impact on things in the future.

The complex interaction between the individual, both professionally and personally, and the environment leads to many factors. Four main themes have emerged from research in terms of what will improve treatment success in helping people return to health and to work, and I have seen this in my own work: work capacity, pursuit of an active and fulfilling life, regaining control, and experiencing support. Your past self, had it gone through burnout and back, would want you to know that.

Your Next Action (2 minutes)

Identify a regular moment when you will check in with yourself on how you are doing. For many, this is the moment when they look at their strategic resilience plan. Frequency may vary, but in general, once per week may work; at the least, monthly. But if things are particularly demanding, a brief daily check-in can help you keep focus in the midst of a particularly high-demand phase.

If you are already off work, you are likely working with your health team to bring you back to health. If you have not yet been connected with a registered psychologist, you may want to check with your health team on whether this is an appropriate addition. If yes, then the sooner the better.

Questions for Reflection

- What is one action you can take the next time a colleague needs to be off work for health reasons?

- If you were to need time off work for health reasons, what would you make sure you did or kept in mind?

Remember

- You have to know the problem; the more you know, the easier it is to see the need to act.

- The individual is on the line (in this case, you), so you need to take realistic actions to prevent and recover.

- Increasing mental health literacy is helpful for you individually and for us all as a professional community. When an opportunity to increase your mental health literacy arises, take it. If no opportunity arises, create one by seeking training.

—[9]—

Build
Team Resilience

Simone is a senior partner in a private equity firm. He and his team are very seasoned and work extremely efficiently. Recently, they worked on a unique and complex deal. Structuring it required them to work with several other teams within their larger organization—teams and experts that were housed in other parts of the organization, some located in other countries. The process was arduous. Each team brought their absolute A-game to the table as they worked to create something none of them had done before, knowing the entire organization had eyes on them. They were all the best at what they did, and they all felt thrilled to be part of this project.

And they delivered. But after the deal closed, they were exhausted. Not just because the project was demanding in itself, but because of the incredible inefficiencies and frictions that they had to work against along the way, the frustration they generated (and that they had no time for), and just how they had gone through the challenges as a group of teams as opposed to a broader team. Each individual and each team was generally fairly resilient on their own; as they joined on this deal, however, it turned out to be a different story. Being at the leading edge of their industry was what they did, and venturing into new territories like this was going to happen again. They had to approach it differently next time.

Look for the Constellation

Team resilience is not defined as a group of individuals with high resilience. It is the constellation of a team's (or teams' if multiple teams are working together) behaviors that allow them to persist, go through adversity, and grow.

Everyone on a team can increase the team's resilience. If you are the leader of a team, you have even more impact. You are also in the role of overseeing the vision, strategy, and culture of your team, creating an environment that promotes creative ideas and supports growth, even out of mistakes. This is critical, because as you foster stability and adaptability, you support sustainable innovation.

Teams vary based on several characteristics, including temporal stability (the team has worked together before and continues to do so), level of task interdependence, life span, virtuality (the team members work in different locations), and many other factors.

Yet all teams need psychological safety, which initially emerged as the psychological equivalent to physical safety in the workplace: the conditions that allow work to be performed in a healthy and safe way. Specifically, psychological safety is created by conditions that at a minimum ensure individuals won't be punished or humiliated for speaking up with concerns or questions or about mistakes. At best, these are conditions that promote psychological health and prevent psychological harm at work. The reality is that all teams will have conflicts. And when these happen, we have to ensure there is enough trust to have good conversations. This supports investment in the factors listed above.

The ways this translates will differ. Particularly when the demands are high, one concrete action may be to increase information about resources available in your organization to increase utilization rates. By taking opportunities that already exist, you minimize how much energy you are expending and are contributing to the organizational resilience. For example, if a team member expresses interest in training and a program exists, or if someone mentions needing more balance and your company offers wellness-focused benefits, you could support them.

If you are bringing new teams or a new configuration of individuals together, erring on the side of communicating more rather than less on your common goal may help. This could be implemented by having frequent overall team touch points during which the common goal and progress toward it are discussed.

Especially when people don't have the benefit of a history of working together, it is critical to focus specifically on creating conditions for psychological safety. It can be as simple as adding a "psychological safety" agenda item to your next meeting, commenting positively on an interaction during which a team member responded with a growth mindset to a challenge, sharing with the group a mistake that you made and how you learned from it, or, as suggested by a study by researchers Constantinos Coutifaris and Adam Grant (a best-selling science author), sharing criticism you have received.

Simone's "team" had become much larger than his direct reports. It had become the larger group of teams that were involved in this project—a constellation. As he and I debriefed on this situation, he realized that if he could rewrite how this went down, he would reach out to other leaders to proactively and frequently communicate with all the teams both on their common goal and on specific aspects of psychological safety, including for them the importance of sharing any challenges as soon as they are identified so the overall team can help.

Your Organizational Resilience

You can influence your team's resilience if you are in a leadership role, and you can also influence your company's resilience. Most employees in an organization are not specifically in charge of the mental health strategy for the organization. The individuals who oversee it already know what organizational resilience is and how to support it.

For most of us—for you—what is important and useful is to know what is likely happening in that area so you can contribute to the momentum from the role you are in, whether you are in an individual contributor or leadership role. Hayden was in charge of a team, and his overall organization also had a client services department. That department not only strove to exceed external clients' expectations but also to do this with their internal clients, which included Hayden's team. Because he had looked into his company's mental health strategy, he knew that there was a focus on recognition. He, therefore, worked to add his voice to this area of focus and made a point of sharing positive feedback with the client services department regularly.

Your own experience of your employer is a valid place to start because you are your employer's target market for their mental health strategy, if they have one. If they don't, your experience is still a valid place to start. And the same applies if you are a solopreneur, where you're both the strategist and the recipient.

Organizational psychological resilience refers to the ability of the overall organization to go through challenges, persist, and come out even stronger. It typically involves good organizational health practices and culture, low levels of organizational risk, and high levels of employee psychological health and safety. It is important, because it is what allows the organization to adapt to change and continue to innovate, and this can lead to positive outcomes. NAV CANADA, mentioned earlier in this book, is an example of a company with high organizational resilience. For over a decade, they worked to identify the particular sources of supply and demands that their employee population was experiencing, identified workplace mental health best practices, and built and evolved their workplace mental health strategy. This involved a number of actions, including ensuring all the existing resources were communicated about frequently and implementing one of the first internal peer support programs. Because they continuously evaluate the outcomes of their efforts, they have adjusted their strategy and actions over time, and continue to do so.

Markers of organizational resilience include a culture that is both strategic and adaptive. The organization is ready for change, as evidenced by some external focus, anticipation of what may be coming, and confidence. It is also action oriented. This often includes constantly developing their capabilities, collaborating in their action planning, and putting a strong focus and value on executing and sustaining change.

Psychological Health and Safety

The Mental Health Commission of Canada (MHCC) developed a National Standard of Canada for Psychological Health and Safety in the Workplace, which identifies thirteen factors associated with a psychologically healthy work environment.

Even if this standard was designed for organizations, teams often function as small versions of organizations, and at times they need their own strategy.

Here are the thirteen factors:

- Psychological and social support
- Civility and respect
- Recognition and reward
- Balance
- Organizational culture
- Psychological demands
- Involvement and influence
- Psychological protection
- Clear leadership and expectations
- Growth and development
- Workload management
- Protection of physical safety
- Engagement

The MHCC subsequently issued two additional factors specifically for the health care industry, but which more and more apply to many other industries:

- Self-care
- Moral distress

A full team typically focuses on organizational mental health strategy, which is fairly complex and requires deep expertise. But as a stakeholder, your perspective counts.

The MHCC factors can easily guide your next action. The next step may simply be to identify one action that would make sense, given your perspective. You could focus on optimizing a strength or helping with a challenge. For example, you might choose to amplify a factor like growth and development by proposing that team members identify a way they are already growing and a potential new area for development.

If you have access to data, that may inform your direction. If most directions look like good opportunities, then you can use recommendations from academic literature, such as recognition and reward. This one is a good place to start for at least two reasons. First, showing appreciation via recognition is not something that requires a budget—no matter your role, you can give it. Second, lack of recognition has been shown by research to have a significant impact on burnout. It is not the only variable, but it is one of them.

You may also create new supports. One group in health care decided to create what they called a compassion team. This involved a weekly interactive video call where people in different roles could share the challenges they were experiencing and support others in their challenges, whether it be caring for six patients on ventilators in open areas without family support or having to let go of large groups of team members.

Team Resilience Needs Everyone's Contribution

It has been said that in small crises, power goes to the center, and in big ones, it goes to the periphery. In the overall mental health area, I would argue that everyone needs to contribute, and most of the power is in the periphery. Something to take advantage of is the responsibility you have, regardless of your role. The need is so great, and we do need new results. As busy as you are, and as busy as the teams you work with are, movement will require everybody's contribution.

The focus of this book is on your individual resilience, recognizing that you are in a context that can change, needs to be monitored, and needs to be considered. Even if we are not directly in charge of the context, often we can have an impact on it. And whether you are aware of your impact on it or not, the context affects you. The size of your context may appear to be so large that you throw your hands in the air and say, "There is nothing I can do about this; I am not the boss." The reality is that sometimes it's possible to affect a small part of your context, which, at times, has a greater effect than we expect. This is often true, whether you are a small part of a very large company or you are a solopreneur working with contractors as needed.

The more we all look at the various parts of the systems we belong to, the more we may understand the forces at play and, most importantly, identify ways to contribute in a healthy direction. In a work situation, this means exploring the ways in which each of us can lead, regardless of our role, toward more team resilience, which will affect organizational resilience.

Here is the key. We don't want to reinvent the theoretical, research, or organizational wheel. And we don't need to; there is a lot out there already. We have publications and white papers on best practices. This is not a mysterious area. We want to contribute to keeping that wheel moving, and each of us must contribute to its movement. It is particularly important that you do this in a realistic way, given all the other demands already on your plate. The question, of course, is how.

You Just Need to Give Direction

I had the chance to go horseback riding in the British Columbia mountains a few years ago. I had only been on a horse a handful of times in my entire life, but I was game for it. Then, as we got close to the date, I became anxious. What if the horse just went off the path, away from the others and in the mountains? How would I keep myself safe?

When we arrived at the ranch, the instructors taught us a few things about our horses and how to ride them. I had thought I would just sit on one and they would just follow each other. Not here. These are amazing horses, trained to navigate in high mountains where many other animals live. They don't react each time there is a noise or a movement; they respond to very clear directions. And so, when you sit on one (which is a thing for me, as I am 5 foot 3!), nothing happens.

Two instructions were key: 1) spread your weight in three spots—where you sit and in each of your feet, and 2) give the horse direction using the reins (I know, shocking—but I did need the full instructions, trust me), and as soon as they get it, release the tension as a "thank you." And the instructors showed us a few things we needed to know to be able to go up and down in mountains and over rocks and logs. We trained close to the ranch, and as a small group each of us reverted at times to forgetting to give commands. Gradually, we saw the impact of our very small actions on creating the desired response from our horse. We all learned quickly that if we just invested a little bit, it would work, and we would move in the right direction.

In some ways, this experience relates to how we think of team resilience. We each have a responsibility to contribute to movement, even if we are facing many other demands. If we each put in even a few minutes, we'll see movement. You just need to give direction.

If you are in HR, this is right up your alley. If you are not in HR, chances are you've found yourself thinking, "This overall resilience and mental health area belongs to HR." While this is on their radar, if you leave it there, you'll probably see some positive impact, but will it move the whole team toward greater resilience? If you don't contribute by giving your own directions, however small, your horse won't move. If instead you have visibility on HR's strategic plan, and if you take the

We have a
responsibility to
contribute to
movement, even
if we face many
other demands.

———————

lead to align that strategic plan with your own, then you and your team will have more resilience now and in the future.

The bigger issue is that it is not up to HR alone, and it is not up to leaders or team members alone—it is up to everyone. Now more than ever. We have more demands, and supply has not changed much, so we are at higher risk. We need everyone to contribute, and everyone is over capacity. No one has a lot of time, and if we keep things big and complicated, then no one will take any action. But we do have knowledge—no need to reinvent the wheel. We just each need to push it a little bit.

You are sitting on your horse and you have the opportunity to create movement. Only you can give directions to your horse. And when everyone on your team does, you'll move forward.

Part of Everyone's Job Description

To recap, resilience is a constellation of behaviors that allow us to persist and move forward through adversity and grow. Individual, team, and organizational resilience are all related. And resilience can act as a protective factor to burnout, compassion fatigue, and psychological distress.

We need to look at how we can increase team and organizational resilience from any role, whether you are in a formal leadership role or may be in the future, or you are a member of a team. We'll look at a survey of options, from which my invitation is that you pick one next action.

Here are some sample actions based on research and my experience:

- Share with colleagues all your emotions, both positive and less so.

- Invite colleagues and team members to share both positive and less-positive emotions.

- Invite conversations about resilience and how you can increase it.

- Share your resilience strategies.

- Keep in mind that each individual may be in a different phase with different demands.

- Invite conversations about the thirteen main factors associated with psychological health at work and how you can improve them as a team.

- Offer recognition when appropriate.

- End emails with an invitation to ideas and solutions.

- If a colleague expresses a negative bias, ask if they are absolutely certain.

- Express compassion for a colleague.

- Work with your team to identify challenging events in advance, manage them during, and recover after.

- Encourage training on psychological health.

- Include realistic information about stressors in job interviews.

- Incorporate boundary preferences.

- Protect the tasks valued by each individual as much as possible.

- Provide the opportunity to remind the team of the resources they have access to.

You may be thinking, "But I am too busy, and I can't add more responsibilities." Remember that this is a system. We don't need you to start a new project; we just need everyone to contribute a little bit. For you, this means just one action so you can contribute to the movement. If you are a member of a team but not the formal leader, this is the team I'd like you to consider. If you are part of many teams, then pick one. If you are the leader of a team, then you can pick either the team you lead or the team you are a member of with your peers, the other leaders. Picking one will make this reflection more effective.

This may feel far from how you see yourself. For some, you are already what is called an "intrapreneur"—an entrepreneur within an organization. The entrepreneur, in any industry, is typically doing demanding work under high uncertainty and high responsibility. They often struggle with feeling isolated, with low social support and low well-being. So far, similar to what you may be dealing with.

What we know from entrepreneurs who stay resilient is that they actively maintain their self-care and social supports, their own resilience. In their work, they are continuously curious and flexible, and they adjust. As we continue with current and future challenges, we need to combine stability and adaptability so we can foster sustained innovation.

The more we nourish curiosity and a growth mindset, the more we set ourselves up for sustained innovation. If you are in a leadership role, operational needs can sometimes take over. However, you may well be the only person on the team whose job it is to lift yourself above and review your approach to meeting the demands, to proceed with strategy and direction, not just actions. This has always been crucial, but with changing demands it is especially vital that you include resilience actions, for you, for the individuals in your teams, and for your teams and your organization.

Your actions will have an impact on others around you, on other teams, and on the overall organization, and even on the resilience of our society, so that we're all more resilient. This is how we create results.

Your Next Action (2 minutes)

Identify one action you will implement at work in the next few days. It can be something new, or it can be something you already do, but not very often. If you're unsure what to do, consider adding "psychological safety" to your next team meeting agenda, with the objective of starting the conversation on what this means in your team's context and what could be your team's next action on this. You don't need to have the answer; this is going to be a conversation that belongs to the team.

If the conversation stalls, mention you were reading a book on strategic resilience, work performance, and mental health for leaders and professionals. Offer to bring *The Resilience Plan* in, and consider holding a book club, where you could discuss the Questions for Reflection provided at the end of each chapter. This is yet another resource, and it's one you can share.

Questions for Reflection

- What is one action you can take to increase your team resilience?

- Who else could benefit from the message in this book?

Remember

- Individual, team, and organizational resilience are all related.

- Each of us has an opportunity to contribute to the resilience of our team and organization. It is an integrated, shared responsibility.

- All teams need psychological safety: conditions that allow for work to happen in a healthy way.

- Sharing positive feedback can add to psychological safety in the workplace.

- Showing appreciation via recognition is not something that requires a budget, and anyone can give it.

- The Mental Health Commission of Canada developed a National Standard of Canada for Psychological Health and Safety in the Workplace that identified thirteen main factors associated with workplace psychological health.

- We're going to have to navigate change, so we might as well approach it with curiosity and leadership.

- All these actions will have a trickle-down effect, and your contribution can be even greater, in addition to improving and protecting your own resilience and that of your team.

Closing

Early on in my MBA program, we were told to join a day-long class, some of which focused on team building. You know these activities: what organizations do to help people get to know each other and work even better as a team. This massive group of three hundred students was brought together to do a drumming exercise.

Early in the process, the leader asked, "Who wants to be the lead drummer, the one who will set the beat and keep it for the group?"

All of us part-time MBA students looked at each other and didn't say anything. Then, someone from the larger group raised their hand and became the lead drummer, and we proceeded.

Later that day I reflected on what had happened. This individual had come prepared to raise their hand. They had a plan; without knowing what the exercise would be, they knew they were coming to participate, and so they did. The rest of us didn't have a plan; we just showed up and saw what happened. And we ended up being led by someone who had come with a plan—a plan to be active and lead.

This experience made me learn with clarity that if we're going to show up, if we're going to make a difference, we need a personal strategic plan. If you want to show up for your own resilience, you need your custom mental health strategy designed around your personal and professional life. You need your helix. This is what will give you the edge you need.

And you need your plan to be well executed, because a fantastic plan with no action doesn't do much, and random actions with no planned direction often go nowhere. Now you have your plan, custom-designed for your own life— your current sources of supply and demands, your values, and your context. You know how to adjust it over time, and you can do so at any time. You'll always be able to revisit this structure. For now, you've got your first actions that are specific to you, make sense, and are doable. Now you can be the lead drummer.

Acknowledgments

——————

want to thank the professionals and leaders in my professional community, including individuals and audiences, for their brilliance, humaneness, and resilience. Thank you for having shared your experiences with me. You'll find your thoughts, feelings, and behaviors in this book in many forms. Know that your experiences, even when modified, have already inspired many others.

I express my gratitude to a group of workshop participants and advance readers from around the world who helped during the pilot and editing of this book. Your insights have been invaluable. Thank you also to my interviewees: Doris Hawaleshka, BSC, CHRP, PPCC; Cindy Kaczmarek, MSW; Les Kertay, PhD; Julie Menten, MSC, JD; Jaana Rask, MSC, MBA; and Lyne Wilson. Your contributions are enriching the book beyond the quotes, and our conversations were invaluable to me.

Writing a book, as it turns out, has many parallels with training for and running a marathon. In the pre-contemplative phase, while I was also building my business as a professional speaker (my other sport), I was lucky enough to work with

Jane Atkinson, who told me to hold on until I had the space for the book (running). Each time I listen to Jane, it works.

Working with AJ Harper as my developmental editor will remain forever one of my best professional experiences. Working with AJ, her colleague Laura, and the community of writers they bring together is like having the best coaches and running group you can think of. Makes you want to go for the Sunday run even when it's cold, windy, and rainy.

You do all this work of writing the book, and then at the equivalent of 23 miles in a 26-mile marathon, your publisher shows up. You think you're done, but you're not. The entire Page Two team literally cheered me on and supported me with their expertise to the finish line. Having the chance to be joined by such a talented, dedicated team at this crucial time provided me with the energy to cross the finish line even faster.

I wish to thank my entire team, who brings their brilliant minds to everything they do and who keeps everything running even when the demands are coming in fast and furious.

Merci to my parents, Fleurette and Marcel, and my sister, Jo, for their inspiring audacity, and to my husband, Nic, and our son, Alex, for their love and shared passion for being in the mountains. Thank you to my close friends and many others I hold in my heart. You ran parts of the marathon with me, held signs of encouragements, made me drink water, and cheered me on all along. *Merci*.

Appendix A
Daily Resilience Planner

Are you energized or exhausted? More than ever, professionals and leaders today are dealing with increasing and unexpected demands. And high rates of burnout continue to rise. Disability related to mental health is at an all-time high.

When you're exhausted, you can't bring your best to your personal and professional life. Small, poor decisions can quickly add up, making a difficult situation worse.

The solution isn't to put your head down and soldier on. Sometimes, most of the solution is in changing the context. Even when the answer is multi-faceted or external to you, one key part of the solution remains: developing skills and practices that support you. While the challenges themselves may also require your attention, increasing your ability to remain your usual confident, energized self can help you manage the situation.

It doesn't take much. Focusing on just one resilience-building activity a day can make a difference. And that's what this Daily Resilience Planner is all about. It provides focused resilience planning based on research. It's an easy way to anchor a single choice you make each day to build resilience.

Just One a Day: Actions to Increase Resilience

Here's a list of actions shown by research to increase resilience. Your goal, in daily resilience building, is to elevate at least one of these actions from "optional" to "priority" each day. Every day. This list is not exhaustive, but all have been shown by research to help with resilience.

Take Your Daily Natural Anti-Depressant

Physical activity represents such a significant part of our psychological health that in some mood disorder treatment studies, it's been shown to take individuals out of the clinical range for mental health issues. For some, physical activity is comparable to anti-depressants and cognitive behavior therapy. It can improve the ways we think, feel, and behave. Which types of physical activity should you focus on? Research points to three: cardio, strength training, and meditative activities, like yoga or meditation.

Color Your Plate

The research is clear: What we eat can significantly impact our psychological health. Many studies have focused on the Mediterranean Diet, which includes lots of fish, leafy vegetables, and olive oil—the same type of diet that has been shown to protect our physical health.

Buy an Alarm Clock

Protecting your sleep includes decreasing distractions such as electronics. Instead of using your phone as your alarm, use an alarm clock so your phone does not enter the bedroom. The amount of sleep we get on a nightly basis affects how well our brain works, which affects our resilience, among other things. Aim for seven to eight hours of sleep per night.

Drink Less (or No) Alcohol

Alcohol is often seen as an accepted way of managing stress. In some work cultures, it is valued. Yet, it is a depressant with several potential negative consequences for health, including psychological health.

Schedule Social Interactions

Research on the importance of relationships is clear. It shows the negative impact of social isolation, even on physical health. The key is to schedule time with someone you like and keep it in your schedule. Treat it like a specialist appointment or a meeting with your biggest client, and arrange other demands around it.

Explore a New Activity

If you've gone through depression, you know how doing things you used to love may no longer generate happiness. But a big part of treatment is still doing these things, even if your heart isn't in it. It helps you get better. The same is true for building resilience, even if you feel tired and unmotivated. It could be a movie night, baking bread, gardening, painting…whatever activity gives you pleasure. Protect your time for activities you enjoy.

Develop a Growth Mindset

We all have some thoughts that carry a negative bias. These can increase as our resilience drops. We want to catch thoughts with a negative bias and turn them into realistic thoughts. Not positive thoughts, which would still be biased; just realistic. You'll likely still experience negative emotions. But what we're taking out of the equation is the "spin," the unnecessary spiral down that comes with negative bias.

The goal is to be more conscious about your thinking. To question your negative bias, ask yourself:

- Am I 100 percent certain of this?
- Is this what a good friend would say?
- Might there be another perspective on this?

Then answer in a realistic, factual, evidence-based way. The process may force you to look at evidence or test your assumptions. In doing so, you'll minimize this negative bias, change your mindset, and strengthen your resilience.

Your Daily Resilience Planner

We can't control the world or people around us, but we can influence our own resilience, which can help us manage tough situations. One aspect we can control is to take the lead on one or two resilience-building actions each day. And these daily actions are what can help us feel stronger, more resilient, and more energized to take on challenges.

So, plan for a daily resilience-building activity. Do it the night before, or first thing in the morning. Here's how to do it:

- Get a notebook (my recommendation) or an erasable marker and white board if you prefer.

- Write down the action(s) you're going to take today (thirty seconds).

- At the end of your day, review the action(s) you had listed and note a win and a lesson (thirty seconds). If using a white board, note these somewhere permanent before wiping the slate clean.

- Repeat the same process the next day.

- At the end of each week, extract the best win(s) and lesson(s); at the end of the month, do the same for the past four weeks (one minute each).

Appendix B

Strategic Resilience Plan Activity Sheets

The following activity sheets include prompts for written exercises. Grab a notebook and pen or open a blank document on your computer and use the answers to these prompts to help inform the Your Next Action exercises at the end of each chapter.

These activity sheets are also available as fillable forms that you can download from drmarie-helene.com/book.

....

Activity Sheet 1: Supply/Demands Inventory

Timeframe:

My sources of supply:

My sources of demands:

Activity Sheet 2: Priority Values List

My values and two or three actions for each:

Values I will focus on as Step 1:

Activity Sheet 3: Quadrants of Context

Personal Context

What is easy:

What is a challenge:

External Context

What is easy:

What is a challenge:

Activity Sheet 4: Custom Strategic Resilience Plan

Goal:

Strategic Pillar 1:

Actions:

Strategic Pillar 2:

Actions:

Strategic Pillar 3:

Actions:

Example Strategic Resilience Plan

This example will give you a sense of how the plan can work.

....

Activity Sheet 1: Supply/Demands Inventory

Timeframe: 1 year

My sources of supply:
- anytime I do a physical activity
- time with my partner
- time with my child
- considering volunteer board work regarding a cause meaningful to me
- interesting clients at work

My sources of demands:
- amount of work and demands at work
- opportunities to help many organizations (too many)
- grief I am going through due to three losses this year

....

Activity Sheet 2: Priority Values List

My values and two or three actions for each

Physical activity:
- swimming
- biking
- running

Family:

- going to a museum with my partner
- doing activities with my child that they like
- stopping work earlier to be with my family

Intellectual challenges:

- having interesting projects
- selecting out projects I prefer not to have when possible
- reading on international travel

Influence:

- expanding my leadership role
- engaging in informal mentoring
- taking on a governance role in a charity

Values I will focus on as Step 1:

- Physical activity, family, and influence

....

Activity Sheet 3: Quadrants of Context

Personal Context

What is easy:

- work (am in a senior role I love)
- love physical activity (not hard for me)
- can be very straightforward

What is a challenge:

- saying no
- tend to put my head down and work
- I can miss many days of exercise and not notice

External Context

What is easy:

- pool close by
- partner supportive of my activities

What is a challenge:

- work culture focus on "yes"
- frequent work travel makes schedule, energy, availability variable

....

Activity Sheet 4: Custom Strategic Resilience Plan

Goal: Increase my resilience

Strategic Pillar 1: Physical activity

Actions:

- On my calendar, schedule realistic amount of activity time daily and monitor it
- Swim once per week, sometime between Monday and Wednesday, six a.m.
- Weekend activity: one or two; bike or hike
- Two weekday thirty-minute activities (at lunch if not in the evening)

Strategic Pillar 2: Boundaries at work

Actions:

- Inform others of my commitments after work and maintain
- Put alarm on my phone and stand up when it rings
- Honest conversation with boss regarding my goals

Strategic Pillar 3: Involvement aligned with my values

Actions:

- Take steps to join non-profit that connects with my values
- Share with boss type of role I am seeking next within the organization
- Daily planning that includes both work and personal commitments on my schedule to protect the latter

About the Author

Marie-Hélène Pelletier ("MH") is an award-winning workplace mental health expert, psychologist, advisor, executive coach, and speaker. She's one of a handful of work psychologists holding both a PhD and MBA, both from the University of British Columbia. Over the course of her career, she has worked with thousands of professionals and leaders and led workplace mental health strategy in senior leadership roles.

Pelletier draws from what clients call a "clear mastery of the subject matter." Her goal is to inspire participants to take action and get results. She brings a mix of business and clinical expertise, translating research about health, performance, resilience, and overcoming challenges into strategies professionals, leaders, and their teams need to thrive.

Pelletier has won numerous academic and industry awards, including the Industry Leadership Award from Benefits Canada, where the organization noted "her credentials make her uniquely suited to help guide the continued evolution of psychological health in the workplace." Connect with her at drmarie-helene.com.

Bring *The Resilience Plan* to Others

———

Inspiring others to build their resilience in both their work and personal lives and take proactive steps is a powerful way to create positive change. Here are four ways you can contribute to this movement:

Engage in meaningful conversations with your team, friends, or book club: Use this book to facilitate purposeful and actionable discussions and inspire your team, friends, or book club to design their own resilience plan.

Share the message within your organization: Contact me about bulk discounts and special offers, including custom editions for special events, which can include a foreword from your CEO and a message from me. A shared message influences a culture and can inspire collective action.

Invite me to speak at your event: Bring me in as a keynote speaker, panel moderator, or workshop facilitator, and I'll bring my energy, passion, knowledge, and humor to inspire participants with new insights and easy takeaways that create results. Visit drmarie-helene.com/speaking for more information on how I can contribute to your event's success.

Partner with me for executive and professional coaching: Work with me to help you gain clarity even faster on your goals and provide you with tools to face particular challenges, navigate transitions, and achieve your professional aspirations. Visit drmarie-helene.com/advisory-coaching to explore how I can support your journey.

Join the Conversation

Connect with me to discuss any of these options for your team or organization or yourself. If you found value in *The Resilience Plan*, help me spread the word on social media with #TheResiliencePlan so that together in our work and personal lives we embrace the power of even more resilience.

Follow me:

in drmhpelletier

⊙ drmhpelletier

▶ youtube.com/@marie-helenepelletier2706

Contact me:

⋈ drmarie-helene.com

✉ mh@drmarie-helene.com